Shifting the Blame

How Victimization Became a Criminal Defense

Saundra Davis Westervelt

Rutgers University Press
New Brunswick, New Jersey, and London

Library of Congress Cataloging-in-Publication Data

Westervelt, Saundra Davis, 1968–
    Shifting the blame : how victimization became a criminal
defence / Saundra Davis Westervelt.
        p.   cm.
    Includes bibliographical references and index.
    ISBN 0-8135-2583-7 (alk. paper). — ISBN 0–8135–2584–5 (pbk. :
alk. paper)
    1. Victims of crimes. 2. Abused women—Psychology. 3. Crime—
Sociological aspects.   I. Title.
HV6250.25.W47   1999
362.88—dc21   98–15629
                                                                    CIP

British Cataloging-in-Publication data for this book is available from the
British Library

Composition by Colophon Typesetting

Manufactured in the United States of America

Shifting the
Blame

To Steve Nock

So far as I can see, *everyone* who achieves anything of note reports having had a mentor, someone to whose spark of encouragement and teaching [she] owes [her] achievement.

Veraswami

Contents

Acknowledgments

The writing of this book has proven to be an incredible learning experience. Of course, I have learned a great deal about the research and book-writing processes, and about the law and the society in which we live. More importantly, though, I have learned that to accomplish anything of merit in any arena of life you must surround yourself with people who are intelligent, creative, and supportive. In this regard, I consider myself extremely lucky. Over the past few years, I have benefitted from the help and support of a number of people—all of whom have contributed to the successful completion of this book. Although I have tried to express my appreciation to each of these individuals, I welcome this opportunity to once again say "thank you."

Most of the work on this book was done while I was a graduate student at the University of Virginia and was made possible by the Bonnie L. Booker-Tate Fellowship Fund and the university's sociology department. I would especially like to acknowledge the assistance of the library staff at the University of Virginia Law Library. At Virginia, I am indebted to Daphne Spain, Gianfranco Poggi, Sharon Hays, Stephan Fuchs, Milton Vickerman, Jim Nolan, and Jeff Tatum for the bibliographical references and useful insights they provided during numerous conversations. Thanks also to Joan Snapp and Kim Nash for letting me "blow off steam" when needed. A special "thank you" to Paul Kooistra at Furman University for inspiring a young sociology undergraduate to take a direction that has proven to be so challenging and rewarding.

Whereas my colleagues at the University of Virginia saw me through the bulk of the project, my new colleagues at the University of North Carolina-Greensboro have been incredibly supportive. I am especially grateful for the encouragement and friendship extended by David Pratto, Julie Brown, David Mitchell, and Jack Humphrey. Steve O'Boyle has provided some much needed assistance tracking down leads and retrieving materials.

Both Dorothy Zellner at the Center for Constitutional Rights and Elizabeth Bochnak at the National Jury Project took time to share their firsthand observations about these two organizations and their roles in the development of the battered woman's self-defense strategy. The reviewers of the initial manuscript—Kevin Delaney and Richard Delgado—raised important questions and pointed out lapses in the original argument; in doing so they made this a far better analysis than it would have been otherwise. The importance of their contributions and assistance cannot be overstated.

I must thank everyone at Rutgers University Press who has supported this project, particularly my editor Martha Heller. Her input has made this a better manuscript and me a better writer, and during the process she has become a trusted friend and colleague.

Throughout this process, I was fortunate to be in the company of very strong, intelligent women whose emotional and intellectual support continually "fueled the fire." To Beth, Karin, Monica, Jill, and Jennifer, I extend a heartfelt "thank you" for everything. During my graduate years, I also benefitted from a dissertation committee that showed sustained interest in and dedication to my ideas. Steve Nock was a friend and mentor from the beginning of my graduate career. I owe him a great deal, only part of which is for his guidance in this project. I thank Sarah Corse and Peggy Plass for their friendship and for showing their confidence in me as a scholar and teacher. I greatly appreciate the insights of Gresham Sykes, who was kind enough to take time out from his painting (and retirement) to share his thoughts with me. Finally, I thank John Monahan for squeezing me into his busy schedule and continuing to provide information and assistance even after I left the University of Virginia. This project is made stronger by incorporating the ideas of someone who has one foot in the social sciences and one foot in the law.

As always, my profoundest gratitude goes to my family, particularly my parents, who have provided unwavering love and support from day one. They taught me many of the things that really made the completion of this project possible—curiosity, dedication, and perseverance. I especially thank my husband Van for being there every step of the way, for helping me find my own path, and for his willingness to walk down that path with me.

Shifting the Blame

1

Responsibility and the Culture of Victimization

In January 1994, two criminal court cases seized the national spotlight. In Los Angeles, the first murder trial of Lyle and Eric Menendez had finally come to an end when the juries announced that they were hopelessly deadlocked, forcing the judge to declare a mistrial. At approximately the same time, on the other side of the country, in Virginia, the jury in the trial of Lorena Bobbitt decided that she was ruled by an "irresistible impulse" when she cut off her husband's penis, acquitting her by reason of temporary insanity. Some people were enraged by these decisions while others were delighted. Despite the varied reactions to the outcomes of these trials, one thing was obvious: something about these two cases had touched a national nerve.

In many ways these cases were very different. The Menendez brothers were accused of murder, Lorena Bobbitt of assault ("malicious wounding"). The brothers claimed a version of self-defense, Bobbitt temporary insanity. The brothers were children (though some would disagree) who attacked their parents; Bobbitt was an adult who assaulted her husband. Yet in spite of these many differences, the two cases shared one main feature: in each, the defendants claimed that they acted as they did because they were victims and that their victimization should excuse their crimes.

In their trial, the Menendez brothers never denied that they killed their parents, having riddled them both with bullets as they sat watching evening television. Instead, the brothers claimed that they were merely shielding themselves from certain injury and possible death at the hands of their parents, most particularly their father. During their trial, the brothers recounted a long history of physical and sexual abuse, painting a portrait of themselves as lifelong victims. The "monsters" said to have inflicted this constant torture were their parents: Jose Menendez through his brutality and Kitty Menendez through her passivity and complicity in his behavior. The brothers claimed that on the evening of the murders they were acting in self-defense. Because of the years of abuse to which they had fallen victim, they believed themselves to be in danger of suffering further abuse or even death. Rather than allowing themselves to be victimized yet again, they decided to strike first—a "preemptive strike" of sorts—in spite of the fact that they were not being attacked at the actual time of the murders. The brothers argued that their actions were justified, or at least partially so,[1] because this past victimization caused them to believe that they were in imminent danger and should strike first to protect themselves. Because the victimization was not their fault, the murders could not be their fault either.

The Bobbitt defense made a similar claim. In her trial, Bobbitt described numerous incidents of physical and sexual abuse inflicted on her by her husband, John, throughout their marriage, including on the night of the incident (though not at the actual time that she assaulted him). She contended that as a result of these years of victimization, she temporarily "lost it"— "blanked out"—and struck back at her abuser, severing his penis with a kitchen knife. The premise of her defense was that she should be excused from responsibility for the assault because the years of victimization she endured caused her to temporarily lose control and act as she did. Because the victimization was not her fault, the assault could not be her fault either.

Thus, these two cases shared the same premise: the defendants were not criminals—murderers and assailants—but innocent victims whose victimization shaped, even caused, their eventual actions, innocent victims who should not be held responsible for actions that were not their fault. The public seemed sharply divided on the legitimacy of this claim. Some sympathized with the defendants and even reveled in the "popular justice" they eventually exacted by attacking their attackers. Others demanded that "victims" be treated the same as others in the criminal justice system and argued that past victimization was unrelated to issues of guilt and responsibility. Still others could not decide what they thought.

Legal scholars seemed equally divided over the legitimacy of the "new" defense strategy. Alan Dershowitz, arguably America's most visible defense attorney, labeled the strategy "the abuse excuse" and warned us that this was an indicator of an increase in "vigilante justice," a move toward lawlessness (Dershowitz 1994b; see also Dershowitz 1994a). Others took the opposite stance, arguing that the victimization defense was an anomaly, a last-ditch, rarely successful effort by desperate defense lawyers (Slade 1994).

To a social scientist, questions about the legitimacy of the defense—whether it should or should not be allowed in court— are not of primary concern. This, after all, is a judgment call, an assessment of the "rightness" or "wrongness" of a particular legal strategy. However, other questions about the use of this strategy come to mind, questions that had gone not only unanswered, but in many cases unasked: "If this is a 'new' defense, as many say it is, then when did it develop?" "How was it first used?" "How is it being used now?" "What is it about this 'abuse excuse' that is making everyone so upset?" "What does it mean for our society that a new defense based on victimization can now be used successfully in court?" All of which, of course, beg the question, "What exactly *is* the 'victimization defense'—the 'abuse excuse'—anyway?" This book originated as an effort to answer these questions.

Since the 1970s, several sociologists and social critics have noted the increase in individuals claiming to be victims and then using that status to relieve themselves of responsibility. These researchers have focused on the entrenchment of this tendency in such institutions as medicine, education, and civil law (Glendon 1991; Hughes 1993; Olson 1991; Peele 1989; Rieff 1991; Sykes 1992a). The fundamental premise of this "culture of victimization" is that victims are innocent bystanders: they are not responsible for the harm that has befallen them. According to the victimization culture, it follows then that victims should not be held accountable for any actions that result directly from their victimization. For example, Peele (1989) notes that the growth of the addiction industry, the expansion in behaviors "treated" within the disease model of addiction, relies on this basic tenet of the victimization culture. When a behavior is labeled as an addiction rather than as misconduct, the individual becomes a victim who suffers from a disease, rather than a deviant or criminal. Actions resulting from the addiction are attributed to the power of the disease, and the actor is "treated," rather than punished. In other words, the individual's status as a victim reduces his free will and level of responsibility. As a result, responsibility is often mitigated or even nullified.

The Bobbitt and Menendez defense strategies relied on this same premise: victimization should mitigate responsibility. In these trials, the defenses told stories of victims, not offenders—innocent people who had been terribly abused by those close to them. Each defense argued that the defendants' actions could be attributed to this abuse; therefore, the defendants should be excused from responsibility for those actions and shielded from punishment.

These and similar recent cases raise important questions about individual responsibility in our society: whom do we hold responsible for their actions? Has our understanding of responsibility changed? Are victims of abuse being added to the ranks of those that we, as a society, excuse from responsibility, along with the insane, the very young, and those under duress? I examine these larger questions through an analysis of the criminal law, focusing specifically on the development and use of the "victimization defense strategy," or "abuse excuse" as it is more popularly known. As such, I use the law as a lens through which to elucidate and assess larger changes in cultural understandings of responsibility.

I choose the law as the primary mechanism for viewing broader understandings of responsibility for a number of reasons. Law, after all, pervades our lives and provides the general rules by which we pattern our behavior. Laws embody community values and attitudes, and often change in accordance with these values and attitudes (Vago 1994). Stated simply, law is "one way of declaring what is morally right and wrong" (Macaulay et al. 1995:5). Changes in law, then, can be interpreted as a signal of broader cultural changes.

In addition, law is an inherently conservative institution, particularly inflexible and resistant to change (Vago 1994). Because our system is based in part on case law, judges in criminal courts look to past cases, or precedents, to determine present judgments. In many ways, this preserves the status quo. If courts have begun to accept new defense strategies based on victimization, this may indicate a broader shift in cultural attitudes about victimization and responsibility.

No wonder, then, that the Menendez and Bobbitt cases captured the nation's attention. More than two unusual cases, these trials became an arena in which our society's most fundamental understandings of responsibility were being debated.

The Culture of Victimization

Several commentators have noted the increased tendency in our society for people to claim victim status and then use that status as a means of alleviating individual responsibility (Birnbaum 1991; Goldberg 1994; Leo 1988, 1990; Morrow 1991). They have labeled this cultural tendency "the culture of victimization." These critics lament that victimization has become an excuse from responsibility, a condition that infringes on free will and reduces the degree to which victims can be blamed for their actions. Aside from the commentary by these social critics, some social scientists have also addressed the growth and impact of the victimization culture and its relationship to individual responsibility, focusing particularly on the medical industry, the university campus, and the law, specifically the civil law (Etzioni 1993; Glendon 1991; Hughes 1993; Olson 1991; Peele 1989; Sykes 1992a).

In these commentaries, the "culture of victimization" refers to the proliferation in American society of individuals and groups claiming the status of "victim." While this expansion in claims to victimhood has centuries-old historical roots (Amato 1990; Sykes 1992a), the entrenchment of this more modern culture of victimization is generally considered to have begun in the 1960s and 1970s. In many ways, the therapeutic, civil rights, and women's movements that flourished during this period relied on the rhetoric of victimhood (Kaminer 1995; Nolan 1998; Rieff 1987; Ryan 1992). Victim status was claimed for those suffering from the effects of racism, sexism, and physical abuse. Two decades later, however, society's victims include those who suffer from practically every conceivable biological malady, psychological infirmity, or social injustice. Recent examples of today's victims include those suffering from lookism (a prejudice against the unattractive), caffeinism (an overdependence on caffeine), chronic lateness syndrome, Clerambault-Kandinsky syndrome (lovesickness), and addictions to everything from narcotics and food to sex (Sykes 1992a; Leo 1990; Sykes 1992b; Leo 1992b; and Olson 1991 respectively).

Yet the culture of victimization goes beyond a mere increase in the number of people claiming victim status. It also refers to the tendency to use victimization as a justification, excuse, and explanation for wrongful behavior and personal irresponsibility. According to this cultural ethos, victimization confers innocence on its claimant, an innocence secured by having suffered some injustice. The victim may elude responsibility because of this implied innocence. Thus, when misconduct is born out of injustice and innocence, the individual—the victim—is not responsible and cannot be blamed (Magnet 1995; Steele 1990). According to the tenets of the victimization culture, our society does not recognize the possibility of "guilty victims" (Kaminer 1995:23)—the two terms are becoming mutually exclusive.

Most of the discussion about the culture of victimization has come from social critics who have lamented the onslaught of the "don't blame me" culture and the resultant demise in personal responsibility they believe it has triggered.[2] These critics write articles with titles such as "Crybabies: Eternal Victims," "The It's-Not-My-Fault Syndrome," "A Nation of Finger Pointers," "Victims All?", and "Don't Blame Me!" They also frequently discuss the popularity of this topic on talk shows such as *Donahue*, *Montel Williams*, and *Sally Jessy Raphael*, which highlight the abused, mistreated, and wronged individuals of our society (see, for example, Gregory 1994; Leo 1994).[3]

While the culture of victimization has received ample attention from the popular press,[4] it has not received equal attention in the social scientific literature. A few studies have examined the impact of the victimization ethos on social institutions though the scholarly literature is generally thin (see Etzioni 1993; Glendon 1991; Hughes 1993; Olson 1991; Peele 1989; Steele 1990; Sykes 1992a. See also Bonnie 1995; Falk 1996; and Wilson 1997 for analysis of the impact on criminal law). While limited in number, these studies do provide some evidence of the gradual entrenchment of the victimization theme in many social institutions.

Victimization—A New Excusing Condition?

Are victims becoming a new category of people excused from responsibility, as the proponents of the culture-of-victimization thesis would lead one to believe? Are we seeing a fundamental shift in our society's most basic beliefs about the nature of individual responsibility? Answered simply, "yes" and "no."

Over the past thirty years, the conditions under which individuals are held accountable for their wrongful behavior have shifted somewhat. As a society, we have begun to accept a new category of individuals who are absolved of responsibility—victims. Victimization has to some extent become a new excusing condition,[5] a new circumstance that relieves one of blame and responsibility for misconduct.

Changes in the criminal law can be used as an indicator of this broader social change. Law, after all, codifies what is going on in society at large, ways of thinking and doing; it provides "a view of the way things are" (Geertz 1983:184). As such, the introduction of victimization as an exculpatory condition within the context of a criminal defense, as in the Menendez and Bobbitt cases discussed earlier, illuminates a similar shift in cultural understandings of individual responsibility. An analysis of the development and expansion of a defense based on victimization "tells the story" of a society that has accepted victimization as a new way of explaining and excusing misbehavior. Like the insanity defense, which established a new condition—mental illness—that excused individuals from responsibility for their misconduct, the victimization defense strategy has established victimization as a new excusing condition.[6]

Also like the insanity defense, the victimization defense strategy has met with only limited success. In other words, not every defendant claiming a mental illness is actually relieved of responsibility, nor is every defendant claiming to be a victim so relieved.[7] The victimization defense strategy is most successful when used by defendants who have been physically abused by individuals some time in the past. These defendants often can document a history of abuse through medical records and eyewitness testimony. They then contend that the history of abuse is causally related to their present misconduct. However, defendants claiming to be victims of more abstract forms of abuse, such as social deprivation, urban decay, or war trauma, are rarely successful in reducing criminal responsibility.

The change in the criminal law, then, is modest but significant. Even though limited, the success of the strategy over the past thirty years established victimization as a new condition that, under certain circumstances, can relieve an individual of criminal responsibility. While significant, this change in no way indicates that every defendant can reconstruct herself as a "victim" in the courtroom.[8] Judges and juries limit who can and cannot be a successful victim in court. When taken as an indicator of larger social changes, this modest change in the law speaks to a society that is struggling with the "victim" status, struggling to determine the meaning attached to victimhood. Under certain circumstances, victimization has become an acceptable "story" to tell, an acceptable way to explain, and possibly excuse, one's behavior.

The second question posed earlier asks: "Are we seeing a fundamental shift in our society's most basic beliefs about the nature of individual responsibility?" While it is true that a shift has occurred, however modest, in our understanding of whom we hold responsible for misconduct, this does not portend the demise of free will or individual responsibility. The victimization defense strategy does inject a form of social determinism into the criminal law ("the abuse I suffered made me do it"); however, psychological and biological determinism have long been recognized within criminal law without significantly shaking its free-will foundations. The limited use and success of the victimization defense strategy highlight the extent to which the free-will model of behavior is still the working hypothesis of the legal system and the foundation for our more generalized understandings of responsibility. In other words, we have not abandoned the free-will model of behavior for determinism; we have simply expanded our notions of those who should be excused from accountability according to that model.

Law as a Window

This analysis of the interaction between law and culture relies heavily on Durkheim's ([1933] 1984) perspective on the law. Durkheim used the law as a window into the broader society, an empirical indication of cultural attitudes and practices (see also Giddens 1972; Lukes and Scull 1983).[9] This has been a highly disputed position within the sociology of law, sparking controversy on a number of fronts. In essence, Durkheim's view assumes two debatable positions. First, Durkheim argues for the "social dependence of law," rather than for legal autonomy (Friedman 1985). Traditionally, this has been a debate between social scientists who advocate for social dependence and legal scholars who argue for autonomy. In agreement with Friedman (1985:28), I contend that these opposing poles are actually best understood as a continuum: "At one pole is a concept of law as totally autonomous; at the other, a concept of law as totally dependent on society. Probably no jurist of any importance would be located at either extreme, although some would lean much more to one side, some to the other."

I lean in the direction of social dependence. Thus, the working framework of this analysis is that law is bound to and impacted by "outside" social forces. Law is not debated, made, and meted out in a social vacuum. Later in this book, for example, I explain how the successful implementation of the victimization defense strategy resulted from the convergence of three such outside factors. First, feminist lawyers and social scientists developed the strategy and advocated for its use in battered women's self-defense cases, making the strategy a new and viable alternative argument in such cases. Second, these entrepreneurs established an organization to support these advocacy initiatives and garnered resources to fund their efforts. Finally, all of this activity took place within a particular social landscape where arguments and ideologies of the women's movement became a focus of public attention. To a great extent, the prominence of the women's movement made possible the successful efforts of the advocates and the support they received. In addition, the feminist reformers drew heavily on the themes of the women's movement—themes of gender equality, sex bias, and victimization—when arguing for the use of the strategy for battered women. This analysis clearly exemplifies the social dependence of law by developing a sociological framework for explaining this particular legal change.

A second controversial assumption of Durkheim's view of law is that changes in culture produce changes in law, often called his "reflection" thesis. Many suggest that change is effected in the reverse—individuals (elites and grassroots entrepreneurs) effect legal change, which produces social change (Delaney 1992; Dror 1968; Grossman and Grossman 1971; Olson 1991; Weitzman 1985). However, this is for the most part a "chicken and egg" controversy. Undoubtedly, these are mutually reinforcing and simultaneously occurring processes; only on rare occasions can researchers say for sure which comes first. This analysis begins with the premise that cultural changes in understandings of victimization and responsibility (engendered in the women's movement and the culture of victimization) have become institutionalized in criminal law through the activities and resources brought to the table by feminist advocates. This, then, is not a passive reflection process, but an active process in which specific individuals introduce ideas about the link between victimization and responsibility into the legal arena. However, no doubt feminist reformers who fought for this institutionalization also contributed to the victimization culture by encouraging the further use of victimization as a culturally valid excuse. Does legal change respond to changes in culture? Yes, but it also contributes to cultural change as well.

So we cannot say for sure which came first. However, I do not believe that should prevent anyone from using changes in the law to say something about the larger culture. To be clear then, this analysis develops a sociological framework for explaining a specific type of legal change—the development of the victimization defense strategy—and uses that change to say something about the larger culture in which we live. Law, then, is used as a window into the broader culture.

The "Victimization Defense Strategy": Definitions and Methods

The label "victimization defense" is often used loosely by the media to describe a wide variety of defenses, ranging from premenstrual syndrome to intermittent explosive disorder to battered woman's syndrome.[10] This broad application of the label includes all defenses in which the defendant claims to suffer from any biological, psychological, or social malady. However, this analysis uses a narrower application of the label, referring only to those defendants who focus on repeated past experiences of social victimization to explain their behavior. "Social victimization" refers to those instances in which an individual has suffered injury as a result of social relations or conditions, as opposed to biological or psychological conditions, such as epilepsy or schizophrenia.[11] Examples of cases of social victimization include individuals who have suffered physical abuse, neglect, socioeconomic deprivation, or discrimination (Bazelon 1976a; Delgado 1985).[12] In each case, the cause of the victimization is the action of another person(s). The cause of the victimization lies in the individual's social environment. According to this definition, a defense based on premenstrual syndrome (PMS) would not be using the victimization defense strategy because PMS is rooted in biology—it is not a form of social victimization. On the other hand, a defense based on physical abuse would be relying on the victimization defense strategy because the cause of the victimization is in the social environment. The victimization defense strategy refers only to those cases in which defendants focus on social victimization as the explanation for their (mis)behavior.

The strategies used by the Menendez defense and by the Bobbitt defense would be examples of two recent high-profile cases that relied on the victimization defense strategy. These defenses argued that the past physical abuse suffered by their defendants in some way caused them to commit the crimes for which they were on trial. A third case topping the headlines over the past few years that drew a wealth of attention to this defense strategy was that of Daimian Osby. Osby won a hung jury in his first trial after claiming that he was suffering from "urban survival syndrome" when he shot two unarmed men.[13] Osby's defense contended that growing up in an urban environment surrounded by violence put him in fear of his life, causing him to shoot the two men. Although these three cases differ in the specific type of victimization they claim (physical abuse by Menendez and Bobbitt, urban fear by Osby), they all locate the source of their victimization in the social environment. They all claim to suffer from some form of social victimization and use that claim as the basis for their defense strategy.

Returning to the definition of "victimization defense strategy," this longer label is used in place of "victimization defense" because the latter implies the existence of a separate legal defense, such as self-defense or insanity, which is based on victimization. Instead, the reliance on a defendant's past social victimization as an exculpatory condition is a new defense *strategy* used within the context of existing true defenses, in particular self-defense and insanity. It is not a separate defense in and of itself. Defense "strategy" refers to the method of argument or plan of attack used by the defense attorney. Thus, the victimization defense strategy is a new way of arguing on behalf of the defendant, a new approach to winning an acquittal based on, say, self-defense or insanity.[14] For example, an abused child offers evidence of past physical abuse by his father to explain why he killed his father in self-defense, even though the father was not abusing the child at the time of the murder. Or an inner-city teen offers testimony about the socioeconomic deprivation she suffered as a child to explain the "psychosis" that prompted her to rob another teen (Flaherty 1995). Thus the victimization defense strategy refers to the use of social victimization as a means of explaining why an actor should be justified or a wrongful act excused, and therefore why responsibility should be absolved.

Though many commentators have noted and criticized the increased use of the strategy, none has provided a detailed analysis of its structure. What exactly does it "look" like when argued in a court of law?

The strategy comprises four main components. First, the defense focuses on the social relationships and conditions in the defendant's past, not just on the immediate behavior of the participants involved in the alleged crime. Thus the strategy is primarily concerned with the defendant's past experiences. Second, the defense attempts to establish a pattern of suffering by the defendant or abusive behavior against the defendant. This generally requires that the defense present evidence of physical abuse suffered by the defendant or evidence of the deprivation or discrimination endured by the defendant earlier in life. Viewed together, the first two elements of the strategy are concerned with establishing the type and cause of the social victimization from which the defendant has suffered during his lifetime.

Third, the defense offers expert testimony on the psychological impact of this past pattern of abuse and suffering on the defendant. This is frequently in the form of testimony by psychiatrists or psychologists who diagnose the defendant as suffering from some malady that was caused by the social victimization. Last, the defense attempts to construct an identity for the defendant that is based on victimization, either by continually referring to the defendant's injuries and suffering or by explicitly referring to the defendant as a "victim."[15]

Conceptually, then, this is primarily a defense based on a determinist model of behavior, rather than on the free-will model enshrined in the law and required for criminal responsibility. With this strategy, the defense attempts to explain the questionable behavior of the defendant within the context of her entire life experience and focuses on the defendant's past victimization as the main causal mechanism explaining her behavior. By establishing the defendant as a victim, the defense associates her with innocence, rather than guilt and responsibility, and argues that, in fact, the defendant was not the master of her actions.

As a potentially successful argument, this strategy is relatively new on the legal scene. Defenses based on child abuse, spouse abuse, or urban survival syndrome would not have been successful, or even raised with any regularity, fifteen to twenty years ago (Goldberg 1994). Therefore, the question becomes, "Under what conditions was the victimization defense strategy first successful and in what ways, if any, has its use been expanded?"

Although it was offered in a number of different types of

cases during the 1970s, the strategy was first used successfully in battered women's self-defense cases in the late 1970s and early 1980s. Three factors came together at this time to promote the success of the strategy in this type of case: (1) the work of feminist activists interested in legal reform; (2) the organizational support of the Women's Self-Defense Law Project; and (3) the connection of the underlying themes of the strategy with those associated with the women's movement, a visible and powerful part of the social landscape at the time.

Since its initial acceptance in battered women's cases, the use of the strategy has been expanded in a variety of ways. The approach is now used successfully not only by women but also by men and children. Though initially used in cases in which the defendant and victim had an intimate relationship, the approach has been expanded to cases in which this relationship is more distant. While it was first used in cases in which the defendant struck back at the person causing her victimization (for example, the battered woman kills her abusive spouse), it can now be used in cases in which the eventual victim of the crime was not the primary victimizer (for example, the defendant was abused and later assaulted an innocent third party). Finally, the strategy has been tenuously expanded to cases characterized by a variety of forms of social victimization other than physical abuse; however, expansion on this front has been limited. Thus, over the past few years, the use of the victimization defense strategy has been successfully extended to a variety of cases that are different from the battered woman's cases in which it was first accepted.

The primary data source I use to examine the development and expansion of the victimization defense strategy is appellate court cases. Secondary source materials, such as law review articles and legal memoranda, are also used both to find relevant appellate cases and to explain the legal arguments offered in these cases.

Generally, appellate cases are those in which the defense

disagrees with the outcome of the original trial and requests a review of the case by a higher court. I use appellate cases for a number of reasons. First, whereas trial court decisions are not published and compiled for public reference,[16] many (though not all) appellate cases are. Each appellate jurisdiction publishes a certain number of its cases each year. These decisions are available by computer as well as in hardcover, making it possible to retrieve cases that share certain characteristics. Thus, for all practical purposes, appellate decisions are the only cases available for systematic analysis.

Second, and more importantly, appellate decisions establish law. Whereas the trial court cases establish the facts of a case, appellate cases decide matters of law and are the cases others look to for guidance in matters of law.[17] When trying cases, lawyers cite appellate cases, not trial cases, as support for their arguments, and judges base their decisions on the precedent established by previous appellate cases. For these reasons, these are the types of cases that will be enumerated here to determine the use and success of the strategy in any given context. This, of course, requires an analysis of the case—the defense arguments used and the case outcomes.

Appellate cases, then, are used to determine the first successful use of the victimization defense strategy. In addition, I analyze more recent appellate cases to determine the extent to which the strategy has been expanded into a variety of other types of cases. The analysis of these cases requires an examination of the social characteristics of the defendant and victim, the relationship between the defendant and victim, the type of social victimization suffered by the defendant (such as physical battering, social deprivation, war trauma), and the source of that social victimization. On occasion, a trial case will be discussed as an indication of the expansion of the strategy. However, trial decisions are only used for the most recent cases (occurring within the past two or three years), which have yet to reach the appellate level.

My initial analysis of law review articles resulted in a list of appellate cases in which the defense strategy had first been used in the 1970s.[18] These cases indicated that the defense strategy had actually been offered in three different types of cases at that time—battered woman's self-defense cases, rotten social background cases, and brainwashing cases. In each of these contexts, defense attorneys had systematically offered each of the four components of the victimization defense strategy in defense of their clients. However, detailed analysis of the cases revealed that the strategy had only been successfully used in one type of case—the battered woman's self-defense case. This, then, became the first type of case in which the victimization defense strategy was used and became the model that defendants in other types of cases used when shaping their defenses.

The "success" of the strategy within a given context refers to the degree to which the victimization defense strategy was accepted by practicing lawyers and legal scholars as a legitimate defense argument. This is by no means intended to suggest that all, or even the majority, of cases using the strategy within battered women's cases were successfully defended. Instead, "success" refers to the extent to which judges, lawyers, and jurors recognized the strategy as an acceptable way of telling the defendant's story. Success is measured in two ways.

First, success is measured by enumerating the appellate cases that "accept" the strategy as a valid defense approach, usually indicated by the reversal and remand of a trial case in which the strategy was offered but disallowed by the trial judge. Unlike trial judges, appellate judges do not often determine the guilt or innocence of the defendant; instead they determine when mistakes have been made in the original trial and can return a case for retrial to allow for the mistakes to be corrected. Appellate cases that have been reversed and remanded in order to allow the full consideration of all elements of the victimization defense strategy are counted as "successful" cases in this analysis. For example, when the victimization defense strategy was first used, many trial courts allowed elements of the strategy to be used, but excluded psychological testimony about the effects of past abuse on the defendant. Many appellate courts overruled this exclusion and remanded the case for retrial, thereby indicating that all elements of the strategy should be allowed.

Thus, to reiterate, trial cases are not the unit of analysis because they are not systematically available. As a result, the number of defendants who "get off" or are acquitted because they relied on this strategy cannot be used as a measure of success. Instead, for reasons already discussed, appellate cases are the unit of analysis. These types of cases rarely address the guilt or innocence of a defendant. "Success" then for a defendant in an appellate case is not acquittal but a decision to remand the case for retrial to allow the use of the complete victimization defense strategy.

The second measure of success is the number of law review articles that specifically focus on the use of the strategy within each context. The number of articles written, both positive and negative, is indicative of the degree to which those in the legal community consider the use of the victimization defense strategy a viable method of argument worthy of discussion. Admittedly, many factors determine the number of articles written about any given subject; however, interest in the subject by professionals in the field is one of these factors. While theoretically it is possible that all of the law review articles written on the strategy in a given type of case could be negative, indicating a rejection of its use by the entire legal field, this is not the case. In each of the three contexts in which the strategy was initially debated, both positive and negative articles were written. Thus, while the number of law review articles focusing on the strategy is an imperfect measure of success when used alone, it does complement the use of appellate cases as the primary measure.

Finally, law reviews, legal memoranda, and other historical materials are used to develop a sociological framework for understanding why the strategy was initially successful only in battered women's self-defense cases. Thus, the methodology employed in this analysis is a combination of case analysis and a thorough, often historical examination of a variety of secondary source materials.

Structure of the Book

For the most part, the book is organized around specific questions. Each chapter is designed to answer a question regarding the development, use, and expansion of the victimization defense strategy, concluding with a consideration of the broader meaning of this legal change for society in general. Chapter 2 is the sole exception to this general structure. This chapter focuses on the legal formulation of individual responsibility and defines the important legal concepts and terms that will be used throughout the rest of the book. The legal elements necessary for the defenses of self-defense, duress, and insanity are explained, as are the legal requirements for the admittance of expert psychological testimony. In addition, the chapter introduces topics such as the "battered woman's defense," the "reasonable person standard," and "brainwashing." This chapter is intended as an accessible overview of the legal concepts that form the foundation of the arguments that follow.

Chapter 3 is developed to answer the question, "When and in what type of case was the victimization defense strategy first used successfully?" This chapter examines the use of the strategy in the three types of cases in which it was first offered in the 1970s—rotten social background cases, brainwashing cases, and battered woman's self-defense cases. An example of the implementation of the strategy in an illustrative case is discussed for each context. For example, the details of Patricia Hearst's famous brainwashing defense are explained to illustrate the de-

fense's use of each of the components of the victimization defense strategy within that context. Finally, the success of the
use of the strategy in each context is documented, indicating
that the strategy was only accepted in battered women's self-
defense cases.

Chapter 4 addresses the question, "Why was the strategy
accepted in battered women's cases but rejected in rotten social background and brainwashing cases?" This chapter provides a sociological framework for explaining the success of the
strategy in battered women's cases, a framework that emphasizes the extralegal factors that promoted its use and success
in that context. Three factors converged to influence the successful implementation of the strategy in these cases. First,
feminist lawyers and social scientists used the strategy to promote gender equality in the application of self-defense law. Second, the Women's Self-Defense Law Project was formed to
provide the necessary resources and personnel to support the
efforts of these feminist entrepreneurs. Third, these efforts and
resources were made possible by the prominence of the
women's movement, as the themes of gender equality, sex-role
stereotyping, and female victimization developed in the strategy relied heavily on the ideologies of this movement. These
advocates, backed by a formal organization with a firm resource
base, drew on the themes that were part of the larger culture
at the time to develop a specific legal argument. In turn, this
promoted the further use of such arguments by those inside and
outside the legal arena. Thus, elite entrepreneurs, formal organizational resources, and resonance within this social landscape are the primary explanatory factors accounting for the
successful implementation of the strategy in battered women's
cases. Theoretically speaking, law and culture interact to en-
courage the use of victimization as an excusing condition.

In chapter 5, the question posed is "How has the use of the
victimization defense strategy expanded since its initial success in battered women's cases?" The use of the strategy has

been extended in three primary areas: the identity of the defendant, the relationship between the defendant and her eventual victim, and the type of social victimization from which the defendant claims to suffer (though expansion in this last area is limited at best). Recent appellate cases indicate that the strategy can now be used successfully by men and children, as well as women. Other cases have relied on the approach on behalf of defendants who have killed or assaulted innocent acquaintances or even strangers. For example, the defense initially was used by those who killed intimates who had been the source of the defendant's abuse. However, the strategy has now been offered by defendants who are abused but kill or assault innocent bystanders who are friends or even strangers. Finally, the strategy has been used by defendants who claim to suffer from a form of social victimization other than physical abuse, such as war trauma or social deprivation. However, again, the successful expansion of the strategy into these types of cases is tenuous. By far the most successful use of the strategy is by defendants who have been physically abused.

Chapter 6 provides a brief review of the arguments developed throughout the book regarding the institutionalization of the new strategy and examines the broader cultural significance of this legal change. The successful establishment of the strategy sheds light on a cultural shift in understandings of *who* is excused from responsibility for misconduct while also pointing to limitations in the magnitude of that shift. In other words, not all victims are excused, only certain victims in certain situations; thus the free-will foundations of legal and moral responsibility are upheld. In this instance, law is instructive as to shifts in cultural understandings of responsibility, but it is also instrumental in defining the meaning of victimization in our culture.

By using this legal change as a lens into our culture, we also see a society struggling with new definitions of personhood. As feminist reformers fight to put forth a model of the equal, rational woman within the battered woman's self-defense strategy, they successfully inject the woman's perspective into the law. Through this new approach, feminist advocates open the door to the legal recognition of more diverse perspectives. If their argument is that a judge and jury cannot understand a woman's actions without looking at the situation from her perspective, then certainly this argument can apply to anyone— people of different races, ethnicities, and cultural backgrounds. The institutionalization of the strategy, then, marks not only a number of moments of redefinition but an increasing movement toward subjectification in the law, which could potentially make the law more accessible to a diversity of voices. Thus, while the extent of legal change itself may be modest, the implications of that change may be far-reaching.

2

Responsibility

under the Law

Individuals deal with questions of responsibility every day. "Who made that great play?" "Who stole my money?" "Who (or what) ate my homework?" From the smallest slight or courtesy to the greatest achievement or most heinous criminal act, people want to know who deserves the credit or blame—who is responsible. Responsibility entails a moral or legal accountability for one's actions (Glover 1970; Ross 1975). In general, responsibility accrues to individuals who "intentionally, negligently, or faultlessly cause harm or benefit" and are therefore deserving of "praise, blame, punishment, and legal pressure to make compensation" (Feinberg 1970:vii). Responsibility is the ability to answer for one's actions and live up to one's obligations.

While individuals can be held responsible for both good and evil, benefit and harm, and can therefore be deserving of both praise and blame (Feinberg 1970), the focus here is primarily on the assignment of blame—individual responsibility for wrongful actions. Under what conditions are individuals held responsible for their misconduct, for their harmful behavior? One way to answer this question is to look to the law as the moral voice of the community (Dressler 1987; see also Durkheim [1933] 1984). Laws do, to some extent, embody the moral values held by any given community at any given time. Therefore, legal rules governing the assignment of individual responsibility and punishment indicate, in many ways, the "social rules" by which people are assigned blame and responsibility (Ross 1975). The legal conditions under which individuals are held accountable for their misconduct are of great importance in understanding how any moral system works.

The Law on Responsibility

The law distinguishes between two kinds of wrongful actions: private wrongs and public wrongs (see Dressler 1987 and Sykes and Cullen 1992 for the following discussion). Private wrongs are harmful actions committed against individuals and are treated under civil law. Civil wrongs generally result in some form of compensation for the injured party, but not in a formal punishment passed down by the state. Public wrongs, on the other hand, are harmful actions committed against society (or the state as society's representative). These are wrongful actions that violate the "public interest" or cause "social harm" and result in some form of state-imposed punishment. Public wrongs are treated according to the criminal law. The focus here will be on the rules of *criminal* responsibility, since they best "articulate the circumstances under which it is morally appropriate to blame and punish persons for committing morally wrong and harmful acts" (Dressler 1987:vii). Civil law is primarily concerned with compensation, whereas criminal law is concerned with moral responsibility and blame.

Given this focus, fundamental to any understanding of responsibility in twentieth-century America is the free-will model of behavior. According to this model, individuals can only be held accountable for their actions (criminal actions in this case) if that conduct is freely chosen, rather than the product of factors external to their will (Dressler 1987; Weinreb 1986). In other words, "If a person does not freely choose behavior, it does not 'belong' to the individual and neither does the . . . blame that may result from the behavior" (Sykes and Cullen 1992:39). If, on the other hand, an individual's misconduct is "determined" by outside factors, rather than freely chosen, that person may be only partially accountable or even fully absolved of responsibility. The law allows for such circumstances, for instance in cases when the perpetrator is insane or under duress from someone who forces the perpetrator to commit a crime.

Free will, then, serves as the cornerstone of the legal system and the assignment of individual responsibility. As Dressler (1987:295) summarizes: "We make moral judgments about people. We condemn people who commit crimes. We blame them for their wrongdoing. At the same time we applaud courage; we praise those who perform acts of benevolence. These reactions are unjustifiable unless we acknowledge the concept of free will—that people can and do choose to do good or to do evil, that human behavior is not scripted by other persons or by non-human forces."

Working within this model of behavior, the law outlines four conditions necessary for the attribution of criminal responsibility.[1] Again, a consideration of these legal conditions required for the assignment of responsibility can provide a guide to society's more general understandings of responsibility and blame. First, an individual must commit a voluntary act (as opposed to merely thinking about committing a crime). This is known as the *actus rea* or the "guilty act" (Hart 1968; LaFave and Scott 1986). Conduct that is involuntary is not a result of free will or rational decision making, and is therefore not legally or morally blameworthy (Dressler 1987).[2] Second, responsibility is assigned only to those individuals who intentionally engage in the *actus rea*.[3] This is the element of *mens rea* or having a "guilty mind" (Hart 1968; Sykes and Cullen 1992). An individual is accountable and morally blameworthy only if she meant to engage in the harmful action. Third, the act must produce "social harm"—some form of injury to individuals or society. This can include direct forms of injury such as murder, as well as more generalized types of injury such as driving while intoxicated, which produces fear and endangers others (Dressler 1987). The final necessary element is causation. An individual is held accountable for his misconduct only when a direct causal connection can be drawn between the individual's actions and a harmful result (Dressler 1987; Feinberg 1970). The voluntary act must produce social harm. Thus, intent, a voluntary act, social harm, and causation are traditionally the conditions that must be met for someone to be held responsible for wrongful behavior and subsequently punished.

In order to convict and punish an individual for committing a particular crime, the prosecutor must convince the "factfinder" of the case, which may be a judge or jury, beyond a reasonable doubt that these four elements occurred simultaneously. The primary role of the prosecution is to present evidence proving the existence of each of these four elements.

This brief examination of the legal rules of criminal responsibility reveals a great deal about society's beliefs concerning the nature of individual responsibility and blame. Generally, we view behavior from a free-will perspective, and therefore assign moral responsibility to those people who cause harm intentionally and voluntarily. We do not hold individuals responsible for behavior that is beyond their control or is unintentional. However, in most cases, we expect individuals to be accountable for their misconduct and often exact punishment as a "formal and solemn pronouncement of the moral condemnation of the community" (Dressler 1987:1).

Given this general expectation, the law does allow for certain circumstances under which individuals are absolved from responsibility for their misconduct. These situations are equally illustrative of the conventional understanding of responsibility and blame in our society (see Dressler 1987 for the following discussion and a more detailed legal explication of criminal defenses). In general, an individual can defend himself against criminal prosecution in two ways: by offering evidence that negates one of the above-mentioned conditions necessary for criminal responsibility (a "case-in-chief" or general defense), or by offering a "true defense" (or affirmative defense).

Case-in-Chief Defenses

Case-in-chief defenses are defenses in the loosest sense of the term. In using this defense tactic, the defendant attempts to negate one or more of the four elements of criminal responsibility that make up the prosecution's case-in-chief. The purpose of such a defense is to raise a reasonable doubt as to the existence of *mens rea, actus rea*, social harm, or causality. The prosecution cannot win a conviction unless all four of these elements have been proven beyond a reasonable doubt (Dressler 1987).

Suppose, for example, that a hunter shoots and kills a fellow hunter whom he, in all honesty, mistook for a deer. In such a case, the defendant—the hunter—could argue that he did not have the requisite *mens rea* for the crime of homicide. He did not intend to kill the other hunter; it was an accident. The prosecution, therefore, would have difficulty proving the existence of *mens rea* beyond a reasonable doubt. Another example of a case-in-chief defense would be the case of an epileptic who struck another person while in the throes of a seizure. The defendant in such a case could offer evidence that her action was involuntary, thereby negating the necessary element of a voluntary act.

In the early 1970s, several legal scholars and one appellate court justice debated whether conditions of social adversity, severe economic deprivation, and childhood trauma ("social victimization") could be used as case-in-chief defenses (Bazelon 1976a, 1976b; Delgado 1979, 1985; Dressler 1979; Gross 1973). Those who favored the use of this form of the victimization defense strategy argued that such extreme conditions limit free choice and impair normal mental functioning, thereby rendering behavior essentially involuntary and individuals incapable of developing *mens rea* (Bazelon 1976a; Delgado 1985). Some of these same scholars also argued for the creation of a new "true" defense, akin to the insanity defense, that would recognize the influence of these kinds of social victimization (Delgado 1979, 1985).

True Defenses

True defenses are those defenses that can result in the acquittal of the defendant *even if* the prosecutor has proven all elements of the crime beyond a reasonable doubt. A true defense does not negate an element of the crime; instead it offers evidence as to why the defendant should not be held responsible for the crime in spite of the presence of all of the elements (Dressler 1987). The law allows for four types of true defenses; in this discussion, though, I will limit myself to the two most important types that relate to the use of the victimization defense strategy—justification and excuse defenses.[4]

Historically, a justified actor and an excused actor were treated differently. The former was acquitted whereas the latter was still punished. In current practice this distinction has been blurred, and justified and excused actors are in most instances treated the same by the criminal justice system (Dressler 1987; Greenawalt 1984). A few situations are still recognized in which the designation of an act as justified or excused may be important in deciding technical legal issues. For example, the distinction is important in determining the legality of third-party conduct. In other words, the lawfulness of assisting an individual who appears to be in trouble can depend on whether that individual's behavior is justified or excused. An individual who helps someone kill an aggressor in self-defense is engaging in lawful behavior because self-defense is a justification defense. However, an individual who helps an insane actor kill someone is engaging in unlawful behavior because insanity is an excuse defense.[5] Other scholars argue that maintaining the distinction between these two concepts is important because they reflect moral judgments about appropriate conduct (Greenawalt 1984, 1986; Robinson 1982).[6]

A justification defense defines conduct that is considered criminal to be socially acceptable under certain circumstances. Justified actions are actions that society encourages or at least tolerates (Dressler 1987). Therefore, in certain cases, conduct that would normally be considered criminal is redefined as the correct and morally appropriate response to a situation. For example, self-defense is a justification defense. Although intentional killing of another human being is usually considered a crime, killing in defense of self is, under limited circumstances, justified—redefined as socially acceptable and permissible. As a result, the actor who kills in self-defense is relieved of moral responsibility, even though all elements of the crime have been proven. Other justification defenses include defense of others, defense of habitation and property, law enforcement, and necessity.[7] Self-defense is the only justification defense that will be discussed in detail because the first successful use of the victimization defense strategy occurred primarily within the context of this defense.

Unlike a justification defense, an excuse defense admits that the act in question is wrong, inappropriate, and unjustified, but the actor is nonetheless not morally to blame for committing the act. For example, a defendant claiming an insanity defense does not deny that all elements of the crime have been proven beyond a reasonable doubt; instead he claims that he lacks moral blameworthiness because he suffers from a mental disease or defect (Dressler 1987).[8] In this case, the actor's behavior is not viewed as the morally appropriate response to the situation (in other words, the act is not justified), but it is excused nonetheless because of the actor's mental deficit.

Other examples of excuse defenses are duress, involuntary intoxication, and immaturity. Again, because of their relevance to the development of the victimization defense strategy, the excuse defenses of duress and insanity will be the primary focuses here.

In sum, a justification defense is universalized while an excuse defense is individualized (Fletcher 1978). A justification defense can apply to any person who finds herself in a similar situation; any person who defends herself against unlawful, imminent aggression will be able to mount the justification defense of self-defense. Excuse defenses, on the other hand, apply only to a particular individual in a particular situation. Another individual in a similar situation would not necessarily have access to an excuse defense. For example, insanity is an excuse only for that particular individual in the commission of that particular act. It is not available to everyone who commits that act.

Although some legal experts have debated the creation of an entirely new defense based on victimization, the strategy has so far been used solely within the context of existing defenses, both justifications and excuses (Delgado 1979; Dressler 1979). The use of the strategy in battered women's cases, for example, has been used to support claims both of self-defense and insanity. An earlier, and less successful, use of the strategy in brainwashing cases was argued within a duress defense. What follows is a brief explanation of the three defenses most often used in connection with the victimization defense strategy—self-defense, duress, and insanity. This discussion should provide the necessary legal framework for the analysis of the development of the victimization defense strategy that follows, and provide a more detailed look at the exceptions to responsibility that both law and culture allow.[9]

Self-Defense

Self-defense is a justification defense. An act committed in self-defense is permissible and not considered to be morally wrong and worthy of blame. As mentioned earlier, the victimization defense strategy was first successfully implemented by feminist legal scholars within the context of self-defense. To understand how and why these advocates framed the strategy within this defense, we must first develop an appreciation of the legal requirements of self-defense.

The defense of self-defense can be claimed in two situations. It can be used in murder and attempted murder cases in which a defendant asserts a right to use deadly force against an aggressor. Or it can involve a claim of moderate and nondeadly force to defend against such offenses as assault or battery. In most cases, however, self-defense arises within the context of homicide prosecutions.

The use of deadly force against an aggressor is justified only under limited circumstances. In general, five principles apply to the legitimate use of force in self-defense. First, a defendant can claim self-defense only if she is not the original aggressor. In legal terms, an actor cannot use force to resist an attack unless that actor is "free from fault" (Dressler 1987:193). The defendant cannot initiate the events that lead the aggressor to attack her and then claim self-defense. For example, if an individual threatens someone in a bar and provokes an attack, that individual cannot raise a claim of self-defense because she is not free from fault.

Second, the threat the defendant faces must be unlawful and imminent. Therefore, an actor is not justified in using force to resist an attack that is legal, even though the actor may feel himself to be in danger of serious injury. For instance, a suspect may not use deadly force to resist the force used by the police in an arrest. The use of force by the police is legal and justified. However, the "excessive" use of force by the police is not legal. A suspect therefore has the right to defend himself against this excessive use of force because this type of force is unlawful. In addition, the threat faced by the defendant must be imminent. The legal concept of "imminence" is traditionally interpreted to mean "immediate." An imminent threat is one that will occur immediately unless combatted. Thus, the use of deadly force is unnecessary and unjustified unless the unlawful threat is immediate.

The imminence requirement of self-defense law is of particular importance to the development of the victimization defense strategy in battered women's cases. The use of the strategy in these cases often attacks this traditional definition of imminence. Battered women often claim that, based on their past experiences with their abusers, they "know" when a severe beating will occur. Although they may not be facing immediate abuse, they believe that a beating is "imminent" in the next minutes, hours, or days, and thus respond with force to stave off this threat (or certainty, as they see it). The use of the strategy in this type of case requires a redefinition or expansion of the immediacy requirement of self-defense.

The third principle guiding the use of self-defense requires that the force used by the defendant must be necessary to avoid the imminent attack. Because it seeks to safeguard human life, even that of an aggressor, the law requires that one exhaust all avenues to avoid attack before resorting to deadly force. Therefore, if a child attempts to strangle an adult, the adult must attempt to neutralize the child without relying on deadly force. The prosecution could argue in such a case that deadly force is unnecessary for an adult to avoid an unlawful and imminent threat posed by a child.

Fourth, the force used by the defendant must be proportional to the threat the defendant reasonably believes herself to be combatting. The proportionality principle requires that an actor not combat nondeadly force with deadly force. In addition, the actor's right to self-defense depends on his reasonable perception of the situation rather than on objective reality. In other words, an actor may defend himself if he reasonably believes that the threat is unlawful and imminent and his use of force is necessary, whether or not that is actually the case.

The actor is allowed to make a reasonable mistake regarding the actual facts of the situation and still claim self-defense. The "reasonableness" of the actor's perception of the situation is based on what is known as the "reasonable person" standard: would a reasonable person in the same situation have believed that the threat was imminent and unlawful and that the force used in return was necessary and proportional to avoid the threat?

Both the proportionality requirement and the reasonable person standard are important to the later discussion of the use of the strategy in battered women's cases. For example, traditional interpretations of the reasonableness standard hold that "the 'reasonable person' is someone of ordinary intelligence, temperament, and physical and mental attributes. In the context of self-defense law this ordinary person was also often described in male terms—i.e., the 'reasonable person' was a 'reasonable man,' even when the defendant asserting the self-defense claim was a woman" (Dressler 1987:202). Therefore, in many past cases, the reasonableness of a woman's act in self-defense was judged according to how an average man would have perceived the situation. Feminist scholars in the 1970s pointed out that such an application of the reasonable person standard put a woman at a disadvantage when raising a claim of self-defense (Gillespie 1989). When under attack, the average woman, being of slighter size and strength, does not always have the ability to respond to an attack in the same way that a man does. Oftentimes, a woman must use a deadly weapon to fend off what a man might perceive to be a nondeadly threat. From the perspective of a woman, such an act is necessary, proportional, and in self-defense. From the perspective of a man, such an act—the use of a deadly weapon to combat nondeadly force—may be unreasonable and disproportionate. From her perspective, the woman has a legitimate claim of self-defense; from the man's perspective (the traditional perspective taken in these cases), she does not.

Having noted this, feminist legal scholars who developed the strategy for battered women's cases attacked the reasonable man standard. In their view, a woman's behavior and the proportionality of her response in a battering situation should be judged from a reasonable woman's perspective, not from a reasonable man's. This argument required a rethinking of the traditional application of self-defense law.

Finally, many (though not all) jurisdictions also attach a fifth requirement to the use of self-defense. Some states require an actor who is under attack to retreat from the attack if a safe avenue of retreat is available. This principle is in place to protect human life and ensure that deadly force is indeed necessary. However, not all jurisdictions require retreat, and few if any require an actor to retreat from his home or "castle" (Kadish 1976). Thus, in the 1970s feminist defense attorneys began questioning prosecutors' accusations that battered women had a duty to retreat from their homes before responding to the abuse they suffered. They contended that, for the most part, no jurisdictions apply such a requirement to men.

To summarize, self-defense is available only when (1) the defendant is free of fault in the situation; (2) the threat to the defendant is unlawful and imminent; (3) the force used to combat the threat is necessary; (4) the force used is proportional to the threat the defendant reasonably believes herself to be facing; and, in some cases, (5) the defendant has attempted to retreat. Only under these limited circumstances can a defendant raise a plea of self-defense and be successful. And, as has been noted already, the development of the victimization defense strategy for use in battered women's self-defense cases questioned and attacked the traditional application of many of these requirements and initiated a reevaluation of the use of the defense.

Some states recognize the partial defense of "imperfect self-defense." The victimization defense strategy has also been used within the context of this version of self-defense.[10] For example, in the first trials of Eric and Lyle Menendez in 1993, the brothers used the victimization defense strategy as the basis for a plea of imperfect self-defense (Fletcher 1995). Unlike a successful claim of self-defense in which the defendant is completely acquitted, a successful plea of imperfect self-defense results in a reduction of the defendant's conviction from murder to manslaughter. The defendant is not, in such a case, relieved of all responsibility.

A defendant can claim a defense of imperfect self-defense when she "honestly but unreasonably" believes that her use of deadly force is justified given the situation (Dressler 1987:199). In their claim of this defense, the Menendez brothers argued that they honestly believed that their parents were going to kill them. Their parents, they claimed, had been physically and sexually abusing them for years and were planning to kill them. To protect themselves, the brothers struck first in self-defense (Fletcher 1995). However, by pleading "imperfect" self-defense, they conceded that their belief in their imminent demise and use of deadly force was unreasonable when judged according to the reasonable person standard.[11]

Duress

Duress is an excuse defense. Although the conduct committed while under duress is condemned and unjustified, the actor is not held responsible or blamed for the act. Stated simply, a defendant can claim a defense of duress when he is coerced into committing a criminal act. Because he is a victim of the coercion, he lacks a "criminal disposition," and is therefore excused (Dressler 1987:260). Duress can be used as a defense against most crimes with the exception of homicide. However, some states do allow duress as an "imperfect" defense to homicide, resulting in a conviction for manslaughter rather than murder. In the mid-1970s, a few legal scholars launched a campaign to use the victimization defense strategy in brainwashing cases that relied primarily on the duress defense.

Generally, the use of a defense of duress requires that four elements be present. As in the case of self-defense, the defendant must be free of fault. The defendant cannot be responsible for being in the coercive situation. In addition, if the defendant has the opportunity to escape the coercive situation without giving in to the aggressor's demands, the defendant must take that opportunity.

The second element required is an imminent threat to kill or seriously injure the defendant or a family member unless the defendant commits the offense. In other words, if the defendant does not do as he is told, he or a family member will be immediately harmed or killed. The purest example of this element is the case in which an aggressor holds a gun to the defendant's head until he cooperates. Note that the harm threatened must be "bodily harm of an extreme nature" (Dressler 1987:259). Threat of a lesser harm, such as a threat to damage property or a pet, is not sufficient. In addition, the threat must be "imminent"—instantly carried out if the defendant does not cooperate. Threat of future harm is not sufficient. Therefore, a defendant may not claim a duress defense if he commits a criminal act because an aggressor threatens to kill him sometime in the future.

The final two elements required for a duress defense involve the "reasonable person" standard discussed earlier. The defendant must reasonably believe that (1) the threat is real, and (2) cooperation with the aggressor is the only way to prevent the threat from being executed. As with self-defense, the reasonableness of the defendant's belief is judged according to what an average reasonable person would have perceived in the same situation.

The use of the victimization defense strategy within the "brainwashing" defense—one of the first types of cases in which the strategy was used—primarily attacks the imminence requirement of the duress defense. The brainwashing defense initially was proposed for situations in which an aggressor "uses physically and psychologically coercive techniques over an extended period of time" to "break" an individual and force her to submit to the aggressor's suggestions (Dressler 1987:269). Later, after the actual coercion—"brainwashing"—has stopped, the individual commits a crime at the uncoerced suggestion of the aggressor. Some scholars argue that the individual should be excused by way of a duress defense because the brainwashing made her believe that she was in danger at all times, even when that danger was not obvious to others (see Delgado 1979; Dressler 1979; and Lunde and Wilson 1977 for a debate about this issue). However, others disagree, arguing that such individuals act according to an uncoerced suggestion, not in response to an imminent deadly threat.

The most prominent attempt to use the strategy in such a duress defense was in the kidnapping and bank robbery trial of newspaper heiress Patricia Hearst. After her arrest, Hearst claimed that she robbed while under duress. Though not visibly under threat of injury at the time of the robbery, she argued that months of physical and mental torture convinced her that she should do as she was instructed at all times or suffer severe consequences. Thus, as with self-defense, the use of the victimization defense strategy in the context of duress requires a reevaluation of the traditional application of the imminence requirement.

Insanity

The final true defense in which the strategy is most often used is the defense of insanity. Few areas of law have evoked as much discussion and disagreement as the insanity defense. The courts and legislatures have developed and enacted five different versions of this defense, each drawing severe criticism from legal scholars and mental health professionals alike. Some have even called for the abolishment of the defense altogether (Goldstein and Katz 1963; Morris 1982; Morse 1985).

Dressler (1987) argues that the insanity defense is highly controversial for a number of reasons. First, although the defense is used quite rarely, it is often used in high-profile cases that receive a great deal of media attention and public scrutiny.[12] For example, the acquittal of John Hinckley (who attacked President Reagan) by virtue of an insanity plea drew wide public controversy and disapproval (Morse 1985). Such high-profile cases bring into sharp relief the tension between our desire to punish wrongdoers and our concern for those with serious mental deficiencies. In addition, this defense requires a mingling of law and psychiatry, two professions with vastly different concerns and views of human nature. A certain degree of controversy is inevitable.

Its controversial nature aside, the insanity defense is another area in which defendants can focus on instances of past social victimization to explain their behavior. Take, for example, the recent case of Lorena Bobbitt, who cut off her husband's penis after he allegedly sexually abused her. Bobbitt argued successfully that she was temporarily insane at the time of her act, a temporary break caused by years of sexual abuse culminating in the husband's abusive behavior that evening (Fletcher 1995). Her experiences of social victimization—past sexual abuse—at his hands bolstered her claim of insanity and won her an acquittal.[13]

The insanity defense is an excuse defense founded on the belief that individuals suffering from severe mental defects cannot be held morally responsible for their actions and should not be punished. The defense is quite complicated, and each version of the defense has its own elements and definitions of legal concepts. In addition, states vary according to which version of the defense they use. In spite of this variation, two versions of the defense are most widely used—the M'Naghten rule and the *Model Penal Code* (MPC) test.[14] Thus, when used to support an insanity plea, the strategy must be adapted to the requirements of one of these two tests.

The M'Naghten Rule and Irresistible Impulse Test.

The first insanity defense of importance to the American judicial system was developed by the English House of Lords in 1843 and has become known as the M'Naghten rule.[15] This version of the defense is concerned solely with the cognitive ability (or disability) of the defendant. Legally speaking, an individual is judged insane if "at the time of her act she was laboring under such a defect of reason from a disease of the mind that she: (1) did not know the nature and quality of the act that she was doing; or (2) did not know that what she was doing was wrong" (Dressler 1987:299). This test has received a great deal of criticism for the ambiguity of such words and phrases as "know," "nature and quality of the act," and "wrong." However, one can generally conclude that an individual is insane under the M'Naghten rule if that individual does not know what he is doing, does not understand the consequences of his behavior, or does not understand that what he is doing is wrong.

One of the strongest criticisms of this rule is that it is scientifically outdated. Psychiatrists argue that it does not take into account "volitional capacity," or the defendant's ability to control his conduct. Mental health experts suggest that a mental illness can limit a person's ability to control his conduct even when the person's cognitive abilities are fairly normal. In response to this criticism, some states have added a third requirement to the M'Naghten rule addressing the issue of volitional capacity. Although the language of this new prong (actually added in the late 1800s) varies by state, generally the new rule states that someone is considered insane if, because of a disease of the mind, he "acted from an irresistible and uncontrollable impulse" (Dressler 1987:301). This prong of the M'Naghten rule is known as the "irresistible impulse" test, more commonly called "temporary insanity." Critics of this rule argue that psychiatrists cannot adequately differentiate an impulse that cannot be resisted from one that simply is not resisted.

Model Penal Code Test. The rule established in the American Law Institute's *Model Penal Code* (1985) provides a restatement of the M'Naghten rule and the irresistible-impulse test into the *Model Penal Code* test or substantial capacity test.[16] According to this version of the insanity defense, an actor is excused if "at the time of the conduct, as a result of mental disease or defect, she lacked substantial capacity: (1) to appreciate the 'criminality' . . . of her conduct; or (2) to conform her conduct to the requirements of the law" (Dressler 1987:302). Thus, this version of the test combines the concern over cognitive disability with the recognition of volitional capacity. It has received little criticism apart from what was directed at the earlier versions of the defense.

The victimization defense strategy has often been offered within the context of these versions of the insanity defense. In such cases, defendants offer evidence concerning past abuse, trauma, or suffering to explain lapses in mental capacity or behavioral control. For example, battered women recount past beatings to explain mental breaks during which they attacked their abusers, or war veterans point to horrific wartime experiences to explain recurring episodes in which they believe themselves to be back at war fighting the enemy (when in reality they are facing an innocent victim).

While it is important to have some understanding of these legal defenses for the following discussion of the development of the victimization defense strategy, the very existence of these defenses speaks to our broader, collective understandings of individual responsibility. While we do expect and exact accountability for misbehavior, we also recognize certain narrowly defined exceptions to that accountability. Yes, our society believes that taking another's life is morally wrong and deserving of blame and punishment, unless that killing is in defense of one's life or the perpetrator is mentally diseased. By recognizing these narrowly defined exceptions to the general rules of responsibility, the law reinforces the general applicability of these rules—the requirement of an intentional, voluntary act that causes social harm—to most people in society.

What happens when a defense strategy prompts a reevaluation and expansion of these narrowly defined exceptions? What happens when a new defense strategy succeeds in increasing the categories of people who can claim an exception? How does this legal change impact on legal and cultural understandings of responsibility? These are the questions that drive the rest of this study.

A Word from the Experts

Given its centrality to the victimization defense strategy, a brief review of the rules governing the admission of expert testimony is in order before we move to the heart of the argument. The use of expert testimony by both the prosecution and the defense has always played an important role in insanity cases and is becoming increasingly important in cases using other defenses as well (Baumann 1983). As outlined earlier, experts play a key part in cases using the strategy, regardless of the type of defense being offered. In these cases, experts explain to the jury how past abuse, or social victimization, can influence or cause later criminal behavior.

Judges look to a number of standards when deciding whether to admit expert testimony in a case, and courts vary in their interpretations of these standards. However, courts have generally relied on four admissibility standards when assessing the relevance of expert opinions. Briefly, these standards are: (1) the relevance of the testimony; (2) the sufficiency of the expert's qualifications; (3) the scientific reliability of the testimony; and (4) the probative value of the material.

The experts' testimony must be judged to be relevant to the issues in the case and must be helpful to the "trier of fact" (*Federal Rules of Evidence*, Rule 702, 1989; Schuller and Vidmar 1992). As stated in *Dyas v United States*, expert testimony "must be so distinctively related to some science, profession, business, or occupation as to be beyond the ken of the average laymen."[17] In other words, the issues addressed by the expert must provide jurors with unique information that is beyond common understanding (Raifman 1983). In addition, the expert must be sufficiently qualified by "knowledge, skill, experience, training, or education" to testify about the relevant issues as an authority in a particular field (*Federal Rules of Evidence*, Rule 702, 1989).

Expert testimony regarding battered woman syndrome is an excellent example of the application of these two standards. Beginning in the late 1970s and early 1980s, defense lawyers began to argue for the admissibility of testimony regarding battered woman syndrome.[18] To be successful, they had to convince judges that their chosen experts were well-qualified authorities in this area, either by having conducted scientific research concerning battered women or by having helped battered women through work in shelters, homes, or social service agencies (Macpherson et al. 1981). Given that research in this area was fairly new, finding experts that could pass the qualification standard was often difficult.[19] In addition, defense attorneys had to convince judges that these experts could testify to matters that were unknown to the average juror. Attorneys often had to educate judges about the common myths and stereotypes about battered women as well as about the nature of the syndrome itself, issues about which jurors would be unaware without the assistance of expert testimony (Schneider and Jordan 1981).[20]

The third admissibility test involves the scientific reliability of the information or data about which the expert is called to testify. Actually, the courts have provided two different reliability tests to determine the admissibility of scientific testimony. The oldest and most widely used was issued in *Frye v United States*.[21] According to *Frye*, "while courts will go a long way in admitting expert testimony deduced from a well-recognized scientific principle or discovery, the thing from which the deduction is made must be sufficiently established to have gained general acceptance in the particular field in which it belongs." This test, then, requires that the information, data, or conclusions about which the expert intends to testify must be generally accepted by the majority of the members of the scientific community. In contrast, the standard issued in *Dyas*, as clarified in *Ibn-Tamas v United States*,[22] provides that admissibility is determined by the "general acceptance of a particular scientific methodology, not an acceptance, beyond that, of particular study results based on that methodology." This second reliability test does not require that the information or conclusions be generally accepted, only the methodology upon which those conclusions are based.

Finally, the fourth admissibility standard requires that the probative value of the testimony outweigh any prejudicial effects it could produce (Frazier and Borgida 1992; Schuller and Vidmar 1992). The testimony must only add to the information available to the jurors, not make their decision for them.

The battered woman syndrome also had to pass these two admissibility standards. Especially in those cases tried in the late 1970s and early 1980s, defense lawyers often had difficulty proving the reliability of the research in this area.[23] Research on battered women was just beginning in the mid- to late 1970s and had already provoked a degree of controversy (D'Emilio 1985). Therefore, proving that findings and conclusions about battered woman syndrome were generally accepted in the field, as required by *Frye*, was a stringent test. The second reliability test offered in *Dyas*, requiring that a researcher's methodology be generally accepted but not necessarily the conclusions, was a less stringent test, and, in fact, was clarified in the first appellate case to admit testimony regarding battered woman syndrome (D'Emilio 1985).[24] Finally, the defense attorneys argued that this testimony would only aid the jury in determining the reasonableness of the woman's perceptions of imminent danger (Schneider and Jordan 1981). The probative value of such information, they argued, far outweighed any prejudicial effects.[25]

Some variation of these four admissibility standards has been applied to any case that includes testimony from an expert witness since the 1920s. Thus, all of the expert testimony offered in cases relying on the victimization defense strategy has been subjected to these standards, and in most cases has met the necessary criteria.

However, in 1993 *Daubert v Merrell Dow Pharmaceuticals, Inc.*[26] significantly altered these longstanding rules of admissibility. This case put federal judges in charge of determining the scientific validity of expert testimony. Judges can no longer depend on the "general acceptance" principle established in *Frye* but are granted the power to assess the validity of testimony independently (Faigman and Wright 1997). Some legal scholars contend that, if applied in good faith, this is a more stringent admissibility standard, one that may exclude some types of testimony that were previously admitted (for example, testimony on battered woman's syndrome—see Faigman and Wright 1997). To the extent that this contention is borne out, such a legal change could have a significant impact on the continued use and expansion of the victimization defense strategy. Given the centrality of experts to the strategy, a stricter admissibility test could thwart its use in the future. In fact, this may be the very impetus for the creation of the stricter standard.

3

Deprivation,

Brainwashing,

and Battering

The Beginnings
of a Victim-Based
Strategy

The victimization defense strategy is a method of argument used within existing defenses, such as self-defense and insanity; it was first formally developed within the legal community in the 1970s. This is not to say that victimization had never previously been used as a defense; however, not until the 1970s was it methodically formulated into a strategy that could be used in all cases that share certain features and circumstances.

During the 1970s, the strategy was used in a variety of types of cases. Scholars argued that it could be used to defend the economically deprived (Bazelon 1976a), the coercively persuaded or "brainwashed" (Delgado 1979), and the physically abused (Bochnak 1981a).[1] Attempts to use the strategy within the first two contexts (as a defense for the economically deprived and the coercively persuaded) were unsuccessful. Its use in these situations received limited attention in law review articles at the time and was not recognized in a single appellate case. Though unsuccessful in other types of cases, when used in battered women's self-defense cases the strategy was relatively successful. Numerous law review articles were written and continue to be written on the merits of such a defense, and many appellate decisions have recognized the validity of the strategy in this context.

To understand fully the differential outcomes in the use of the victimization defense strategy, I will review its use in illustrative cases from each of these three contexts, and document the success or failure of the strategy in each context. First, however, I will consider a criticism often directed at those who proclaim the "abuse excuse" as a new defense strategy—the criticism that, in fact, this is nothing new at all (Bonnie 1995).

Determinism and the Law

Is the victimization defense strategy as outlined here truly "new" as some claim (Dershowitz 1994a; Goldberg 1994; Sneirson 1995)? After all, excuses such as "the devil made me do it" and "it's not my fault" are as old as criminal law itself. Shifting the blame is part and parcel of most criminal defenses. Therefore, understanding the victimization defense strategy as a new variation on an old theme requires a brief examination of the role of determinism, especially social determinism, in the law.[2]

Those using the victimization defense strategy attempt to explain their behavior with reference to repeated past experiences of "social victimization." Again, social victimization refers to instances in which an individual has suffered injury as a result of social relations or conditions, such as physical abuse, neglect, socioeconomic deprivation, or discrimination. A defense based on social victimization is different from one based on biological or psychological victimization; in the latter the focus is on the extent to which behavior results from physical or mental illness. However, these defenses do share an emphasis on determinism, a belief that the defendant's behavior is caused by some force or agent other than the will of the individual. Whereas an insanity defense based on premenstrual syndrome or paranoid schizophrenia introduces an element of biological or psychological determinism into the law, the victimization defense strategy introduces a degree of social determinism. In this sense, it is a new defense strategy.

The law is premised on a free-will model of human behavior. Law, especially criminal law, establishes sets of circumstances under which individuals are held responsible for their behavior and punished when they do something wrong. This function of the law would not be justified unless we, as a society, accepted that "people can and do choose to do good or to do evil, that human behavior is not scripted by other persons or by non-human forces" (Dressler 1987:295). Blame and punishment require free will. Generally, law is resistant to the principles of determinism because they interfere with the assignment of responsibility. If behavior is not of one's choosing, blame and punishment cannot be fairly attributed (Norrie 1983).

Historically, however, criminal law has recognized that, in some cases and under limited circumstances, an individual's behavior may not be freely chosen but determined by some force external to individual will and choice. Such arguments have generally been most successful within the context of the insanity defense.[3] Beginning with the M'Naghten rule in 1843,[4] defense law has recognized that a mental disease or defect can produce such mental impairment as to render someone legally insane and, therefore, excused from criminal liability (Skeen 1983). This established an acceptable forum for a defense argument based on biological determinism.[5] Since that time, several biological and psychological conditions have been admitted as bases for successful insanity defenses (Fox 1963; LaFave and

Scott 1986). Conditions such as paranoia, senility, and epilepsy have been proven to impair mental functioning and behavioral controls to the point that defendants have been excused from criminal liability.[6]

Courts have not been as willing to accept arguments based on social determinism—economic deprivation, social injustice, or physical abuse (Bazelon 1976a; Morse 1976). Because it is rooted in a medical model of behavior, only biologically based diseases and defects have been considered to be valid foundations for the insanity defense (Bazelon 1976a). Courts have been reluctant to recognize any determinist argument that is not rooted in this model and based on a proven mental disease or defect (Delgado 1985; Diamond 1973; see also *United States v Brawner*[7]). In fact, defendants who rely on the typical insanity defense are not required to offer evidence of the *causes* of their mental disease—environmental or biological (Morse 1978). For example, in *Commonwealth v Bruno*,[8] the court explicitly excluded evidence offered by the defense regarding the possible societally based causes of the defendant's mental illness. Evidence of the existence of the disease itself was enough; a consideration of the social-environmental roots of the disease was unnecessary and irrelevant.[9]

The formulation of the victimization defense strategy in the 1970s represents a significant departure from past determinist arguments. While the inclusion of expert testimony about the mental state of the defendant is still a key component, the primary focus of the strategy is the *cause* of that mental state. The expert testifies about the psychological impact on the defendant of past abuse, deprivation, or neglect. Thus, the court must consider the cause of the mental state, rather than just evidence of the existence of a mental illness, as in the typical insanity case. This represents both an attempt to expand the medical model to include all factors that may impact on someone's mental state and an attempt to recognize that some mental illnesses are produced by social conditions. As a result, while the strategy can be used within the context of the insanity defense, it has also been used to support a defense of duress (see *The Trial of Patty Hearst* 1976—cited hereafter as *Patty Hearst*[10]) and self-defense (Bochnak 1981a). Therefore, the development and use of the strategy is not only a concentrated effort to introduce social determinism into the law, but also an effort to expand the traditional medical model of human behavior to include socially-based causes of medical conditions.

The victimization defense strategy developed in the 1970s requires judges and juries to consider the social causes of a defendant's behavior, aside from or as the root cause of biological or psychological maladies; to consider whether a defendant's behavior is justified or excused because of abuses and injustices suffered in the past; and to evaluate a defendant's behavior with reference to his entire life experience. Although it is sometimes used within the context of an insanity defense, it is unlike a typical insanity defense case in that the defense is required to present testimony about the causes of the mental disease; for example, the defendant went temporarily insane *because* of the abuse she suffered or the discrimination to which he was subjected. For these reasons, the victimization defense strategy is in fact "new."

Deprivation and Brainwashing: Early Uses of the Strategy

The victimization defense strategy was used initially within three different types of cases during the 1970s. David Bazelon, Chief Justice of the U.S. Court of Appeals for the D.C. Circuit, was the first to propose the use of the strategy in defense of defendants suffering from social, economic, and cultural deprivation (Bazelon 1976a). This version of the strategy became known as the "rotten social background" defense (or RSB defense) after a defense attorney in *United States v Alexander and Murdock* argued that his client "did not have control of his conduct, and the reason for that lack of control was a deepseated emotional disorder that was rooted in his 'rotten social background'."[11]

The famous Patty Hearst trial in 1976 popularized the use of the strategy for a second type of case—the defense of those brainwashed by their captors. In the wake of the trial, Richard Delgado (1979:19) developed a more systematic version of the brainwashing defense based on the victimization defense strategy, claiming its wide appeal for cases involving similar "thought reform victims." Finally, feminist legal scholars used the victimization defense argument as the foundation for a battered woman's self-defense strategy in which the female defendant's behavior is placed within the context of her entire life experience (Schneider 1980; Schneider and Jordan 1981).

The four elements of the victimization defense strategy outlined earlier are present in each of these three types of cases. In each case, defense attorneys attempt to focus on the behavior of others or the social conditions prevalent in the defendant's past. They present evidence of a pattern of continued abuse or suffering experienced by the defendant, and offer expert testimony regarding the psychological impact of the past abuse and suffering on the defendant's present behavior. Finally, the defense attempts to construct an identity for the defendant based on victimization, highlighting the defendant's suffering and often explicitly referring to the defendant as a "victim." The defense thus places the conduct of the defendant within the context of her entire life experience, focusing on the defendant's social victimization as the main cause of the criminal behavior.

Although the defense strategy used in each of these types of cases was essentially the same, the strategy was only successful when used in battered women's self-defense cases; the "rotten social background" and "brainwashing" defenses did not succeed. Again, the success of the strategy in a given context is determined by: (1) appellate court cases that "accept" the strategy used by the defense, usually indicated by a reversal of a conviction and an order to remand the case for retrial (see chapter 1 for a more complete description of this methodology), and (2) the number of law review articles that focus specifically on the use of the strategy within a given context.

Rotten Social Background Defense

Proponents of the rotten social background defense argue that the insanity defense should be expanded to include mental impairments caused by socioeconomic conditions, such as social and economic deprivation and racial discrimination (Bazelon 1976a). As mentioned earlier, the insanity defense only considers impairments rooted in biological conditions. Thus, proponents of the RSB defense argue that the insanity defense should be expanded beyond the medical model, and that the courts should consider all factors that produce mental impairments, not merely biological or psychological determinants (Bazelon 1976a; see also *Washington v United States*[12]).

The RSB defense is premised on the theory that "one's past or early background can mitigate responsibility for one's later actions" (Vuoso 1987). The model for this defense rests on testimony that the defendant is a "victim" of a rotten social background, and therefore suffered from poverty and deprivation over a period of time in the past (Delgado 1985). Coupled with this evidence is expert testimony explaining the impact of such a history of deprivation on the behavior of the defendant—how living in such conditions over a period of time impairs one's behavioral controls and alters one's perceptions of right and wrong (Delgado 1985). This proposed model of the RSB defense includes all of the elements of the victimization defense strategy outlined earlier.

The RSB defense was first raised in a 1973 appellate case heard in the D.C. Circuit Court.[13] This case centered around two black defendants who opened fire on a group of marines after the marines directed a number of racial epithets at the defendants. Two marines were killed, and another marine and a woman were injured. The defendant Murdock entered an insanity plea, arguing that at the time of the incident he was delusional and mentally impaired because of the emotional and economic deprivation and racial discrimination he had suffered as a child. Murdock was found sane and convicted. The conviction was upheld on appeal.[14]

Analysis of the appellate decision reveals that all elements of the victimization defense strategy were used in this case. The defense's theory was that "Murdock had an abnormal mental condition caused in part by his 'rotten social background' " and that this environment "conditioned him to respond to certain stimuli in a manner most of us would consider flagrantly inappropriate."[15] Therefore, Murdock's insanity defense rested on presenting evidence of his rotten social background and the abnormal mental condition that resulted from it.

The defense presented evidence of the social conditions and relationships characteristic of the defendant's childhood to establish a history of emotional trauma. According to the defense, the defendant grew up in the "Watts section of Los Angeles . . . in a large family with little money and little love or attention"; in addition, the defense reported that the defendant had been subject to racial discrimination and, as a result, had learned to mistrust white people.[16] The defense offered expert psychiatric testimony on the impact of such a history of deprivation and trauma on the defendant's later behavior. Dr. Williams, a psychiatrist who examined Murdock, testified that "Murdock was suffering from an abnormal mental condition that substantially impaired his behavior controls. . . . a deepseated emotional disorder that was rooted in his 'rotten social background'."[17] The defense's continued focus on Murdock's rotten social background and "early conditioning" within such a deprived environment clearly established him as a "victim"—someone suffering from an undesirable condition. In fact, in his written dissent, Bazelon refers to the defendant and others in similar circumstances as "victims of a racist society."[18]

Thus, the defense attempts to place the behavior of the defendant within the context of his entire life experience and to draw a causative connection between his past social victimization and present conduct. The victimization defense strategy used by the defense in this case is best summarized by the defense counsel's closing argument:

> Dr. Williams [psychiatric expert] premised his conclusion on the fact that this man had had what we might call a rotten social background. Now we know that most people survive rotten social backgrounds. But most people are not now here at this time on trial. The question is whether the rotten social background was a causative factor and prevented his keeping controls at that critical moment. . . . At the critical moment when he stepped back in the Little Tavern restaurant and he was faced with five whites, with all of his concepts, rightly or wrongly, as to whether white people were the bogeymen that he considered them to be, the question at this moment is whether he can control himself. That is the only question. . . . Now you have got to take the trip back through his lifetime with him and look at the effect that his lifetime had on him at that moment and determine whether he could control himself or not.[19]

The trial judge in this case was clear in his rejection of this defense strategy. When instructing the jury about the legal definition of insanity, the judge added, "We are not concerned with a question of whether or not a man had a rotten social background. We are concerned with the question of his criminal responsibility."[20] As Bazelon notes in his dissent, this instruction has the effect of "telling the jury to disregard the testimony relating to Murdock's social and economic background."[21] Although the judge did allow the evidence of

Murdock's background to be admitted, this admonition to the jury can be taken has a clear rejection of the validity of the defense strategy. As a result, Murdock's conviction was affirmed. The defense strategy was not successful.

Although the conviction was affirmed, Chief Justice Bazelon dissented in part, arguing that the trial judge was in error in giving these instructions to the jury. According to Bazelon, the instruction "clearly undermined Murdock's approach to the insanity defense in this case."[22] Bazelon stated that he would have reversed and remanded Murdock's conviction based on this error, thus providing the first judicial support for a defense based on social and economic deprivation (although his colleagues on the bench disagreed and affirmed the conviction).[23] Bazelon later expanded his ideas on the RSB defense in a 1976 address, arguing that a defense that recognizes the social sources of mental impairment should be legally recognized (1976a).

Bazelon's ideas sparked a heated though short-lived controversy about the validity of such a defense. Only six law review articles that specifically discussed the RSB defense in detail were written between 1968 and 1976.[24] In the mid-1980s, Delgado (1985) stimulated renewed interest in this defense with his detailed analysis of its uses. However, the debate was again limited; between 1985 and 1995 only seven law review articles focused on the RSB defense.[25] No other appellate case arguments relied on this defense at all, much less successfully.[26]

The RSB defense met with no legal acceptance in the appellate courts or in the legal community. It was the focus of only thirteen law review articles, only six of them written around the time the defense was first proposed. Rotten social background was the primary defense strategy in only one appellate case and was rejected by the court in that case, indicating that the use of the victimization defense strategy within this particular context was a failure.[27]

Given the similarities between the rotten social background defense and the "black rage" defense that has captured headlines lately, a brief note about the latter is in order before continuing. As defined by Bazelon (1976a), a rotten social background includes social and economic deprivation *and* racial discrimination; all of these factors were important evidence in support of the RSB defense. However, a few legal scholars during the 1970s argued that a history of racial tension and discrimination should serve as a separate defense called the "black rage" defense (Delgado 1985; Gabel and Harris 1982; Harris 1977).[28] This defense was an attempt to "explain a black defendant's criminal behavior in terms of the oppressive reality of a black person's life in the United States" (Gabel and Harris 1982:403). The term "black rage" was first used by William Grier and Price Cobbs in their 1968 book of the same name. Grier and Cobbs defined black rage as a mental disturbance resulting from "white oppression of blacks" (1968:207). They argued that long-term exposure to racism, injustice, and discrimination caused blacks in the United States to develop a variety of mental impairments, such as paranoia, schizophrenia, and depression.

Attorney Paul Harris, the most vocal advocate for this defense, argued that black defendants should use this concept as the foundation for an insanity defense (Delgado 1985; Harris 1977). He developed a model of this defense that included a focus on the defendant's history of living in a ghetto environment as well as the history of racial discrimination in the United States. An expert would then testify as to the impact of this history of suffering and deprivation on the individual, and that this suffering created a rage in the defendant that eventually exploded and rendered his actions involuntary (Delgado 1985). As with the RSB defense, all elements of the victimization defense strategy are used in this model.

Although a few scholars argued for a separate defense based on black rage (Gabel and Harris 1982), most scholars treat this defense as part-and-parcel of the rotten social background defense, including Harris himself (Bazelon 1976a; Delgado 1985; Harris 1977; Morse 1976). Both defenses require an inquiry into the social background of the defendant. In fact, one of the cases cited by Harris as a black rage case is also cited as the first RSB defense case—*United States v Alexander and Murdock*.[29] As Harris himself writes (1977:93; see also Harris 1997), "The black rage type of defense can be expanded to all races, to both sexes, and to many different situations."[30] Therefore, for the analysis here, the appellate cases demonstrate that the black rage defense is merely a restatement of the RSB defense.[31]

Brainwashing Defense

Brainwashing refers to a "forcible indoctrination process designed to induce the subject to abandon existing political, religious, or social beliefs in favor of a rigid system imposed by the indoctrinator" (Delgado 1979). The indoctrination process includes subjecting the individual being indoctrinated to isolation, degradation, torture, and rigid routines (Davis 1976; Lunde and Wilson 1977). The term "brainwashing" was first used in the early 1950s by American journalist Edward Hunter (1952) to describe the indoctrination techniques used by the Chinese Communists (Lunde and Wilson 1977). The term was popularized during the Korean War to refer to the techniques used by the Communists to force U.S. servicemen to collaborate with the enemy (Delgado 1979; Lunde and Wilson 1977). Brainwashing is also called "coercive persuasion," "thought reform," "menticide," and "forced conversion" by scholars who have researched the process and its effects (Lunde and Wilson 1977).

Before the 1970s, the term "brainwashing" had been used in only one appellate case—*People v Otis*.[32] Despite its popularization at the time, "brainwashing" was not used in any of the court-martial trials of those servicemen who had collaborated with the enemy during the Korean conflict (Lunde and

Wilson 1977).[33] Not until the 1970s did the brainwashing defense, also called the defense of "coercive persuasion," become the subject of much attention and heated controversy within the legal community. The bulk of this new attention resulted primarily from the Patty Hearst trial in 1976.[34]

On February 4, 1974, Patty Hearst was kidnapped from her apartment by members of the Symbionese Liberation Army (SLA), a radical terrorist organization (Lunde and Wilson 1977; *Patty Hearst* 1976). Approximately ten weeks after her abduction, Hearst was videotaped robbing the Hibernia Bank in San Francisco with other members of the SLA. At trial, her attorney, F. Lee Bailey, argued that Hearst had been tortured, sexually assaulted, and kept in a closet during her period of captivity while being continually read SLA propaganda. As a result of this constant torture and indoctrination, she was in constant fear of her captors, and thus committed the robbery while under duress (*Patty Hearst* 1976). Bailey established the importance of brainwashing to Hearst's duress defense within the first few paragraphs of his opening statement:

> Laymen like to call it brainwashing. . . . Donald DeFreeze [SLA member] knew just enough about this process to start it moving and had for himself a particularly vulnerable, frightened—for obvious reasons—19-year-old girl. And the program was to persuade her over a period of time that she had been abandoned by society, her parents, and all of law enforcement. They had become her enemy and, ultimately, that they would kill her if she exposed herself or tried to turn herself in. (*Patty Hearst* 1976:6–7)

This case initiated a debate within the legal community about the validity of the brainwashing, or coercive persuasion, defense. The basic premise of the defense is that a captor uses "physically and psychologically coercive techniques over an extended period of time in order to render [a subject] submissive" (Dressler 1987:269). Then, much later, the "victim" commits a crime at the "uncoerced suggestion" of the captor (Dressler 1987:269–270). In essence, the subject is under the control of the captor even when the captor is not present or being coercive. The subject is convinced of the captor's omnipotence (Davis 1976).

This model of the brainwashing defense contains all of the elements of the victimization defense strategy. The defense focuses on the defendant's prior experiences, her behavior and the behavior of her captors preceding the actual time of the crime (Dressler 1987). The defense presents evidence of the abuse and coercion suffered by the defendant at the hands of the indoctrinators (Dressler 1987; Lunde and Wilson 1977). The defense presents psychiatric testimony about the impact of the past coercion and brainwashing on the perceptions and behavior of the defendant (Lunde and Wilson 1977; *Patty Hearst* 1976). And throughout their argument, the defense emphasizes the extent to which the defendant is really the "victim," a captive and unwilling participant (Delgado 1979; Dressler 1987).

The brainwashing defense strategy can be used to support an insanity defense. In such cases, the defense would argue that the coercion and indoctrination experienced by the defendant produced an "induced psychosis" that reduced her mental strength and altered her perceptions of right and wrong (Lunde and Wilson 1977). However, in the Hearst case, the brainwashing defense was used to support a duress defense. The defense argued that the torture and isolation she experienced as a captive made Hearst believe that she was in danger at all times. Although at the time of the crime she appeared to be in no imminent danger of serious bodily harm—no one was holding a gun to her head—she believed that she would have been shot if she had resisted participation in the robbery. While a duress defense normally requires that the threat of serious injury be imminent, Hearst's attorneys claimed that because of coercive persuasion "her actions were the involuntary results of duress applied by her alleged captors, the Symbionese Liberation Army."[35]

A detailed analysis of the Hearst trial transcript reveals that all elements of the victimization defense strategy were used to support the defense's brainwashing theory. To begin, because Hearst's duress defense was founded on her claim of the abuse she suffered after her kidnapping, the defense was required to focus extensively and repeatedly on those past experiences and the behavior of her captors toward her. As one of her appellate cases reports, Hearst "described in exhaustive detail the events immediately following her kidnapping of February 4, 1974."[36] This testimony focused predominantly on the way she was treated by her kidnappers. During her four and a half days of testimony, Hearst described "physical and sexual abuses by members of the Symbionese Liberation Army (SLA), extensive interrogations, forced tape recordings and written communications designed to convince her family that she had become a revolutionary, and training in guerrilla welfare."[37]

The following interchanges between Hearst and Bailey are indicative of this testimony (see *Patty Hearst* 1976):

Q: All right. Now, just tell me the sensations that you can recollect when you were being put in what you later discovered to be a closet, just what you remember.

A: I just was really scared, and I guess I must have started to do something, because right away they said—they told me it was a closet. And they just put me in it and closed the door.

Q: All right. Now, I take it, you were still blindfolded?

A: Yes.

Q: Still gagged?

A: Yes.

Q: Were your hands still bound?

A: Yes.

Q: What about your feet?

A: No.

Q: Once the door was closed, was there any light that you could tell through your blindfold, or was it dark?

A: No, it was dark. (154)

———————

Q: What did he [one of the captors] do to you?
A: He pinched me.
Q: Where?
A: My breasts and down.
Q: Your private parts as well?
A: Yes.
Q: And then, did he go back to the closet?
A: Then he left the closet. (158)

———————

Q: When Mr. Wolfe came in the closet, what did he say and do?
A: I don't really remember what, if anything, he said.
Q: Did he take you out of the closet?
A: No.
Q: What did he do?
A: He came in to the closet and he closed the door and—
Q: Did he make you lie down on the floor?
A: Yes.
Q: And then what did he do?
A: Had sexual intercourse.
Q: At some time after that, did someone else come to the closet for the same purpose?
A: Yes. (165)

In addition to Hearst's own testimony about these experiences, three psychiatric experts—Dr. Louis West, Dr. Martin Oren, and Dr. Robert Lifton—also testified on her behalf (*Patty Hearst* 1976). All three had studied the process of coercive persuasion among prisoners of war and testified as experts in this area. Each expert testified that Patty Hearst had been the "victim" of coercive persuasion attempts by the SLA and that she suffered from a "traumatic neurosis" as a result of these experiences (*Patty Hearst* 1976:260, 323). As Dr. Lifton testified, "I have no doubt in my mind that at the time she was arrested, she was suffering from a traumatic syndrome or traumatic neurosis. . . . You know the process of disease, of the syndrome, begins the moment of capture when she's kidnapped. . . . It takes

much more intense form when she's in that closet being subjected to all those humiliations" (*Patty Hearst* 1976:323).

Dr. Oren agreed with this diagnosis, stating, "I would con-
cur with Doctor West and Doctor Singer's view that this is best
termed a traumatic neurosis" (*Patty Hearst* 1976:299). He later
added that, as a result of these experiences and her psychological state, Hearst "was forced to become an outlaw" (*Patty
Hearst* 1976:299). Finally, Dr. West summarizes the impact of
Hearst's captivity on her mental state and motivations for committing the robbery:

> Miss Hearst has still not completely recovered from the
> symptoms of traumatic neurosis that began with a shock,
> being kidnapped 4 February, 1974, battered, isolated,
> blindfolded and confined to the small closet continuously
> for approximately fifty-seven days, tormented, reduced to
> a helpless and physically weakened state, threatened re-
> peatedly with death, sexually molested and raped . . . hu-
> miliated in various ways. For example, verbally shorn of
> her hair and so forth, rendered submissive and highly sus-
> ceptible by the debility and dependency and dread and fi-
> nally left without hope of survival unless she complied
> with all the demands upon her by the SLA and gave the
> appearance of joining the group. (*Patty Hearst* 1976:261)

The final component of the victimization defense strategy
evident in the trial of Patty Hearst is the attempt to reconstruct
the identity of the defendant as that of a victim. From the outset of the trial, the defense continually referred to Hearst as a
victim, thereby redefining her as an unwilling captive rather
than as an active, willing offender. Bailey describes Hearst as a
victim several times during his opening statement to the jury,
for example calling her the "victim of this kidnapping" (*Patty
Hearst* 1976:7). He continues to refer to her as "a victim"
throughout the case, even when questioning the witnesses. For
example, when questioning one of the witnesses to her initial

kidnapping, Bailey asked, "In other words, between the front of the building and the trunk of the car, where the victim ultimately wound up, where were they [SLA members] when you first saw them?" (*Patty Hearst* 1976:148). And again later, he asked, "Do you know how many people you saw besides the victim when you first looked out?" (*Patty Hearst* 1976:149).

Several of the witnesses also used the term "victim" when talking about Hearst. One witness testified, "We saw the victim placed in the trunk of the car, and one of us had called the heat" (*Patty Hearst* 1976:148). Dr. West even used such terminology when comparing Hearst's experiences to those of similar "victims that I had seen in the past" (*Patty Hearst* 1976:253). In her appellate case, the court summed up her case as follows: "The central theme of her lengthy testimony was that from the moment of her kidnapping to the time of her arrest she was an unwilling victim of the SLA."[38] These specific references to Hearst as the "victim" in conjunction with the repeated testimony about the abuses she suffered clearly illustrate the defense's intention to place Hearst in the role of the victim, an unwilling captive who was not in control of her actions and therefore should not be held accountable for them.

Unfortunately for Hearst, this use of the defense strategy was no more successful than its previous use in the rotten social background context. The trial concluded on March 19, 1976, approximately one and a half months after it began. The next day the jury convicted Hearst of armed robbery and the use of a firearm to commit a felony. On appeal, a motion for a new trial was denied, and the conviction was affirmed.[39]

Since the conclusion of this case, a handful of other cases relying on both duress and insanity defenses have attempted to use the strategy based on brainwashing, but with no success.[40] In fact, in an Alabama case that raised this issue (*Neelley v State*),[41] the court ruled that "brainwashing" was an improper legal defense. In a later case (*United States v Fishman*),[42] the court excluded expert testimony on brainwashing, arguing that brainwashing was not fully accepted within the scientific community, and therefore did not pass the test established in *Frye v United States*.[43]

While the Hearst case did spark some discussion in the legal community, the commentary on the defense was limited and short-lived. Only four law review articles were written on the brainwashing defense in the late 1970s and two more in the 1980s (Alldridge 1984; Davis 1976; Delgado 1979; Dressler 1979, 1989; Lunde and Wilson 1977). Thus, as with the rotten social background defense, the brainwashing defense failed in court and was not considered a fruitful defense strategy to pursue.[44]

Battered Woman's Self-Defense: A Successful Defense Strategy

Until the 1970s, battered women who were charged with killing their abusers typically pled "guilty" or "not guilty by reason of insanity" and were routinely convicted (Schneider 1980; Schneider and Jordan 1981; Walker 1993). The legal community's willingness to accept such pleas, with little questioning as to whether there might be an alternative plea, was founded on and reinforced the stereotypes that women who are violent are irrational and mentally unstable (Schneider 1980; Schneider and Jordan 1981). On occasion, women pleading insanity would be acquitted because the jury was convinced that these women were hysterical and "out of their minds" (Schneider 1980).[45]

Women who killed their batterers were rarely acquitted on self-defense. Their actions were rarely construed as justified. This is not to say that acquittals based on self-defense never occurred, but defense attorneys generally relied on an insanity defense, if a defense was offered at all.[46] To some extent, this was the case because the situations in which many women killed their abusers often did not fit the traditional model of self-defense.

Self-defense requires the use of proportional and necessary force in response to a reasonable perception of imminent and serious bodily injury (Dressler 1987). However, many women who kill their abusers do not fit into this model in a number of different ways. First, women are more likely to kill in a non-confrontational situation, when the husband is asleep or not immediately abusing the woman, making it difficult to prove that the danger was, in fact, imminent (Bochnak 1981a; Cipparone 1987; Ewing 1987; Rosen 1986).[47] In addition, these women are more likely to use a weapon even when the husband is not armed, making it difficult to prove that the woman's use of force was proportional to that of her attacker (Schneider and Jordan 1981). Because of these characteristics of the situation—the use of a weapon against an unarmed person in a nonconfrontational situation—the woman's behavior is often interpreted as an unreasonable response to the situation (Gillespie 1989; Schneider 1980; Schneider and Jordan 1981). Because of these apparent contradictions between the situations in which many women kill and traditional self-defense law, these women have been forced to rely on an insanity defense or concede guilt.

In the mid-1970s, feminist legal scholars began to analyze the application of self-defense law as part of a wholesale critique of social institutions, including the law (Chafetz and Dworkin 1986; Vago 1994). These scholars argued that the law was based on a male model of behavior, and thus was unequally applied to men and women (Gillespie 1989; Schneider 1980; Schneider and Jordan 1981).[48] They examined the history of self-defense law and explained that the rules of self-defense developed within the context of the male experience. The typical situation to which self-defense was intended to apply was a confrontation between two men who did not know each other, who were of relatively equal size and strength, and who were socialized and trained in the skills needed to defend oneself (Gillespie 1989). Because the rules of self-defense reflect this typically "male situation," the concepts of "imminent danger," "proportional force," and "reasonable perception of danger" are all defined from a male's perspective.

However, the situations in which many women kill their attackers are quite different from this type of confrontation. Women are more likely to kill within a domestic situation; they are more likely to know their attackers. They are less likely to possess size and strength comparable to their attackers and less likely to be trained in the skills needed to defend oneself (Schneider and Jordan 1981; Schuller and Vidmar 1992). Because self-defense law does not reflect the typical female experience, women in these situations are less likely to have access to the law.

In response to this apparent bias, feminist legal scholars developed the battered woman's self-defense strategy to "overcome sex-bias in the law of self-defense and to equalize treatment of women in the courts" by "recognizing women's different experiences and the different circumstances in which women kill" (Schneider 1986c:197). Specifically, this defense strategy recognizes that "due to a variety of societally-based factors, a woman may reasonably perceive imminent and lethal danger in a situation in which a man might not," justifying her "recourse to deadly force" (Schneider and Jordan 1981:4). Although the situation in which a woman defends herself may be different from the situation in which a man does, her actions may be no less valid and justified. Thus the battered woman's self-defense strategy was an explicit attempt to incorporate "women's experiences and perspectives into existing concepts of criminal law" (Schneider and Jordan 1981:4; see also Rosen 1986:37).

The battered woman's self-defense strategy was initially developed by feminist legal scholars who participated in the Women's Self-Defense Law Project, formed in 1978 to help defend battered women who had killed their abusers (Bochnak 1981a; Schneider 1986b).[49] The defense strategy is premised on the belief that it is necessary to understand a woman's entire life experience with her victim to explain why she reasonably perceived herself to be in imminent danger (Schneider and Jordan 1981). This is especially essential in cases in which a woman kills her abuser in a nonconfrontational situation. The strategy is designed to combat the limitations of the traditional self-defense model when applied to battered women's cases and to make women's justified use of force understandable to judges and juries. The components of the battered woman's self-defense strategy parallel those of the victimization defense strategy.[50]

Traditional self-defense law focuses on the behavior of both participants at the time of and immediately preceding the homicide incident in order to determine if the danger facing the defendant is imminent. Because self-defense law is based on the assumption that the participants in the incident are strangers, they are assumed to have no past relationship relevant to the situation. Therefore, self-defense cases have generally only been concerned with the circumstances immediately surrounding the homicide situation.

This is not the case in the majority of the cases in which women kill their attackers. These women do know their victims and often have a relatively extensive history with them. This history gives them a context in which to understand the behavior of their victims (Schneider 1986c). Therefore, in these cases it is essential for the defense to focus on the victim's past behavior toward the woman in order to understand her perspective and interpretation of his behavior at the time of the homicide incident (Schneider and Jordan 1981). This component of the battered woman's self-defense strategy is the first element of the victimization defense strategy—a focus on the behavior of others in the defendant's past. Because the defendant and her victim have a prior relationship, "the events of recent moments, days, weeks, and months may be admissible to show that the defendant was provoked" and that her actions were reasonable (Schneider and Jordan 1981:24; see also Rosen 1986; Schneider 1980; Thompson 1986).[51]

The second component of the victimization defense strategy involves introducing evidence of the past abuse suffered by the defendant at the hands of her victim. In relation to battered women's self-defense cases, Kieviet (1978:229) states, "evidence of repeated verbal and physical abuse should be viewed as a valuable component in the battered wife's defense." This includes evidence of injuries, trips to the hospital, calls for help, and the victim's reputation for violence (Schneider 1980; Thompson 1986). This evidence is important in developing the context in which the defendant was acting. A history of past abuse helps to explain how the defendant could reasonably perceive that she was in fear for her life (Bochnak 1981b; Kieviet 1978).

Studies show that women in battering relationships learn to recognize certain behaviors or cues that signal the onset of the abuse (Walker 1984). Also, these women learn that their husbands can inflict severe injuries using only their fists and that the women are incapable of fighting back or defending themselves due to their slighter size and strength (Gillespie 1989; Schneider and Jordan 1981). Thus, evidence of past abuse can explain why a woman reasonably perceived the attack to be imminent. Such testimony also helps a jury to understand why a woman may need to use a weapon in her defense, even if it is not "proportional" to the use of fists. She has learned that proportional force, in this case her own fists, is not enough to defend herself against an attack. Evidence of past abuse, then, is essential to the defense strategy because it helps a jury understand why the woman's actions were reasonable and justified in this situation.

The third component of the victimization defense strategy is the use of expert testimony to explain "the cumulative effects of repeated violence" on the defendant (Walker 1984:143). This testimony can establish "the typical effects that such a relationship has upon the state of mind of a battered woman, and the specific effects of that relationship upon the particular defendant" (Cipparone 1987:440).[52] Although not necessarily used in every case, expert testimony is usually given by a qualified psychologist or psychiatrist (Rosen 1986). The presentation of expert testimony can accomplish a number of important objectives. First, it can dispel myths and stereotypes jurors might hold about battered women (Schneider 1980; Schneider and Jordan 1981)[53]—for example, that battered women are masochists who enjoy being abused or who bring it on themselves. Jurors believing such myths would not be able to objectively judge the behavior of the defendant.

Expert testimony can also be used to explain why women stay in abusive relationships, a question jurors may believe to be central to understanding the defendant's motives for the homicide (Rosen 1986; Schuller and Vidmar 1992; Thompson 1986). Finally, experts can explain how repeated abuse shapes the fears and perceptions of a battered woman (Bochnak 1981b; D'Emilio 1985; Walker 1989). Expert testimony can provide a foundation for understanding why a defendant could reasonably perceive imminent danger based on her knowledge of and relationship with the victim (Rosen 1986; Walker 1989). Thus, expert testimony provides a scientific basis for a woman's reasonable perceptions of danger, even when she may not be under immediate attack.

Most, but not all, expert testimony in battered women's self-defense cases is about battered woman syndrome (Rosen 1986). Battered woman syndrome is "a cluster of psychological sequela from living in a violent relationship" (Walker 1984). The concept was first developed by psychologist Lenore Walker in *The Battered Woman* (1979). Her study of women who were in abusive relationships revealed that these women shared many characteristics, such as depression, guilt, and helplessness (Walker 1984).

In *The Battered Woman* (1979) and her follow-up book *The*

Battered Woman Syndrome (1984), Walker argued that many abusive relationships are characterized by a "cycle of violence" that has three distinct phases. In the first phase, called the "tension building phase," the woman tries to "keep the peace" to reduce the possibility of violence occurring. The woman often tries to avoid doing things that have sparked violence in the past. The second phase, the "acute battering incident," is characterized by the eruption of violence. The third phase is the "honeymoon phase," in which the abuser apologizes for his violence and promises never to abuse the woman again. It is this third phase, coupled with external social and economic pressures, that convinces the woman to remain in the relationship. In addition, Walker argued that women who are subjected to continual and random violence suffer from "learned helplessness"; they learn that they cannot control the onset of violence and eventually become passive and unable to respond to or terminate the relationship.

Some scholars argue that expert testimony specifically about battered woman syndrome is essential to a successful battered woman's self-defense case (D'Emilio 1985; Thompson 1986; Walker 1989). This testimony can help explain why an abused woman stays in the relationship, dispelling the myth that she somehow "asked for it," and why she has reason to perceive imminent danger. For the most part, testimony about battered woman syndrome has encountered more resistance from the courts than other components of the victimization defense strategy.[54] Therefore, acceptance of testimony on battered woman syndrome generally signals acceptance of the entire defense strategy.

The final component of the victimization defense strategy is the attempt to construct an identity for the defendant based on victimization, a reconceptualization of the defendant as a victim rather than an offender. Though not explicitly stated, the language used by the legal scholars who developed it indicates that this is a component of the defense strategy. In general, the criticism of self-defense law was part of a broader feminist critique of law that focused on recognizing gender bias in the law as well as on the extent to which crimes of which women are the primary victims—rape, domestic violence, sexual harassment—were ignored or deemphasized (Bochnak 1981a; Mackinnon 1989; Okun 1986; Pleck 1987; Ryan 1992). Thus, the specific criticism of defense law was couched within a broader emphasis on women as victims of sexism, oppression, and crimes such as rape and domestic abuse.

More specifically, however, the feminist scholars who developed the battered woman's self-defense strategy emphasized the extent to which these women were victims of violent men, violent relationships, and a sexist law. The centrality of testimony about the injuries and abuses these women suffered only emphasized and illustrated the extent of their victimization.

In the introduction to *Women's Self-Defense Cases*, the most prominent and direct documentation of the development of the defense strategy, Elizabeth Bochnak states that the strategy was designed to provide "effective representation for women victims of violence who were forced to defend themselves," establishing from the outset of the book the identity of the women as victims (Bochnak 1981a:xv). Again, later in her discussion of case preparation, Bochnak (1981b:68) emphasizes the importance of explaining the "accumulated feelings of rage and fear that come from being a victim of abuse over a long period of time." Elizabeth Schneider, one of the most prominent members of the Women's Self-Defense Law Project, argues that one function of expert testimony is to demonstrate "that the battered woman was a victim" (1986c:202). She claims that the defense strategy in these cases should have two primary themes—the reasonableness of the woman's perception of danger and her victimization: "The critical defense problem in representing battered women who kill and assert self-defense is how to explain the woman's *action* as reasonable. The woman's experience as a battered woman and her inability to leave the relationship—her victimization—is the context in which that action occurs" (Schneider 1986c:199).[55]

The self-defense cases themselves attest to the defense's intention to reconstruct the defendant as the victim. For example, in *State v Hundley* the court writes, "The abuse is so severe, for so long a time and the threat of bodily harm so constant, it creates a standard mental attitude in its *victims*. Battered women are terror-stricken people whose mental state is distorted and bears a marked resemblance to that of a hostage or a prisoner of war."[56] In *People v Powell*, the court explains, " 'Learned helplessness' is identified by defendant as a recently documented theory which explains the psychological paralysis that maintains the *victim* status of the battered wife."[57] Finally, in *State v Kelly* the court summarizes recent research on domestic violence:

> In the past decade social scientists and the legal community began to examine the forces that generate and perpetuate wife beating and violence in the family. What has been revealed is that the problem affects many more people than had been thought and that the *victims* of the violence are not only the battered family members (almost always either the wife or the children). There are also many other strangers to the family who feel the devastating impact, often in the form of violence, of the psychological damage suffered by the *victims*.[58]

Beginning with the first formulations of the defense strategy in women's self-defense cases, the defense aimed to place the defendant in the role of the victim, emphasizing the abuse she suffered and how that abuse shaped her perceptions and behavior. This strategy, therefore, explicitly offered a defendant's past social victimization as the explanation for her wrongful actions and argued for the alleviation of responsibility based on that victimization. Clearly, then, all elements of the victimization defense strategy are used in the context of the battered woman's self-defense strategy. Each element contributes to the overall goal of the defense to explain the homicide situation from the perspective of the woman, a woman whose past relationship to the homicide victim provides a context for her reasonable perception of the situation.

A sample trial brief included in *Women's Self-Defense Cases* (Bochnak 1981a:225–234) illustrates the implementation of this strategy. This brief was written by the defense to argue for the introduction of lay testimony about the character of the deceased as well as expert testimony on battered woman syndrome. To provide a justification for the introduction of such evidence, the brief recounts the defense's entire theory of the case. All elements of the victimization defense strategy are clearly evident.

The brief concerns the case of Eloise Shields, who is charged with the murder of her common-law husband, Sidney Watson. She asserts that the relationship was characterized by abuse and that her husband had beaten her earlier on the night of the homicide. She claims self-defense. As stated in the brief, the defense seeks to introduce testimony about the past behavior of the deceased, his reputation for violence, and his repeated abuse of the defendant, thus incorporating the first two components of the victimization defense strategy. As outlined in the brief:

> We have here a situation where the deceased indulged in heavy drinking both in the past and on the night in question, we have here a situation where the deceased frequently and repeatedly beat the defendant when under the influence of alcohol, and those beatings became more and more frequent and more intense as the relationship evolved. The jury must decide whether or not the defendant acted reasonably under the circumstances. Those circumstances are not limited solely to November 26, 1977,

but to the totality of the circumstances which led up to the slaying of Sidney Watson. (Bochnak 1981a:227)

The brief continues, stating:

> the prior acts of the victim represent a progression of increasing violence toward the defendant, and where defendant's response on the night in question was based upon the cumulative effect of this violence at the hands of the victim. . . . proof of prior acts of violence by the victim which would naturally create apprehension in the defendant is of the utmost relevance. (1981a:230)

The defense also seeks to introduce expert testimony on battered woman syndrome, the third component of the model. The defense argues:

> The anxieties and pressures attendant upon the battered woman syndrome must be shared with the jury if they are to judge and assess the reasonableness of defendant's conduct. Defendant Shields will also have an opportunity to prove her own state of mind, and since the victim's continuous and brutal beatings were an integral part of defendant's state of mind at the moment of the shooting, then testimony with regard to this assault, both as a single event and in the context of numerous other assaults, is relevant to show the reasonableness of defendant's fear and conduct. (1981a:232)

In addition, the defense asserts that testimony about battered woman syndrome is essential to explain how "the battered woman becomes a victim" (1981a:233). The defense argues that both the expert testimony on battered woman syndrome and the lay testimony about the deceased's reputation for violence will help the jury to determine "who was the true assailant and who was the true victim" (1981a:230), insinuating that in such cases these roles are reversed—the victim is in fact the offender and the offender the true victim. The brief concludes with one final attempt to reconstruct the identity of the defendant as the true victim: "the Court should permit the introduction of testimony by Dr. J. Doron on the socio-psychological phenomenon of the battered woman and the defendant, Eloise Shields, as a victim of that phenomenon" (1981a:234).

This brief is included in *Women's Self-Defense Cases* as an example of the type of defense strategy to be used in battered women's self-defense cases, a method of argument to be replicated by other lawyers faced with similar cases. Clearly, this brief illustrates the use of the victimization defense strategy within the context of the battered woman's self-defense case.

The battered woman's self-defense strategy has been used in a number of cases.[59] As with the other two uses of the victimization defense strategy, the use of the strategy within battered women's cases initially met with resistance in the appellate courts. However, unlike the rotten social background and brainwashing cases, the courts did eventually recognize the validity of the strategy within this new context. *Commonwealth v Stonehouse*[60] is an excellent example of an appellate case that supported the use of the victimization defense strategy in a battered woman's self-defense case, reversing the conviction of the defendant because the defendant's trial counsel failed to introduce several of the key components of the strategy.

Stonehouse was a new police officer for the city of Pittsburgh when she met and began dating fellow officer Welsh in March 1980.[61] They dated until October 1980. During those seven months, Welsh continually harassed the defendant by breaking into her apartment, banging on her door late at night, damaging her car, and telephoning her constantly at odd hours. After their break-up, the harassment escalated. Welsh threatened other men she dated, continued to break into her home, destroyed her apartment, and ripped and damaged her clothing. One night after Stonehouse agreed to meet with him in hopes of stopping the harassment, Welsh threw her out of his car, tried to run over her several times, and finally broke her nose by punching her. Stonehouse made several attempts to reduce or end the harassment. She moved several times, stopped dating, and restricted her social activities. In addition, she called the police on several occasions, all to no avail: Welsh continued the abuse and began threatening her with death. This pattern of behavior continued until March 1983. On the day of the homicide in March, Welsh had again followed the defendant and entered her home illegally, this time brandishing a .357 magnum and threatening her with death. After an altercation in which Welsh held the gun to her head, the defendant thought she heard a gunshot and returned fire, hitting the victim twice. He later died. She was charged with homicide. Stonehouse was convicted of third-degree murder and sentenced to seven to fourteen years in prison. The Superior Court affirmed the conviction.

This appeal was brought to the Supreme Court of Pennsylvania. On appeal, the defense argued that the defendant's trial counsel was ineffective on a number of counts, and therefore the conviction should be reversed and remanded for a new trial. The appellate court agreed, claiming that trial counsel had been in error by *not* offering evidence regarding several of the components of the victimization defense strategy.

For example, the defense argued on appeal that the trial counsel had erred in not requesting jury instructions that would require the jury to focus on "the cumulative effects of psychological and physical abuse when assessing the reasonableness of a battered person's fear of imminent danger of death or serious bodily harm."[62] The appellate court agreed, stating that "the jury should have been apprised of the fact that the abuse appellant suffered for three years was to be considered by the jury."[63] In support of this ruling they cited the following passage from *Commonwealth v Watson*: "[Where] there has been physical abuse over a long period of time, the circumstances which assist the court in determining the reasonableness of a defendant's fear of death or serious injury at the time of a killing include the defendant's familiarity with the victim's behavior in the past."[64]

The court concluded that this failure to instruct the jury about the "legal relevance of the history of abuse" was in error.[65] Thus, the court stated as a matter of law that in battered women's self-defense cases the court should require the jury to focus on the past behavior of the deceased and the evidence of past abuse suffered by the defendant at the hands of the deceased.

The defendant also argued that counsel was ineffective in its failure to present expert testimony "regarding the characteristics of the victims of psychological and physical abuse" in the form of testimony about battered woman syndrome.[66] Again, the court agreed, stating that "it is clear that where a pattern of battering has been shown, the battered woman syndrome must be presented to the jury through the introduction of relevant evidence."[67] The court also argued that expert testimony on battered woman syndrome is important because it dispels "erroneous myths concerning the victims of such abuse" and that "uncontradicted testimony revealed that appellant was the victim of such abuse."[68]

The court in *Stonehouse* clearly suggested the importance of each element of the victimization defense strategy to a successful battered woman's self-defense case. What is most significant about this case is that the defense strategy had *not* been used initially at trial. In this case, the appellate court appears to be admonishing the trial counsel for not using the strategy by reversing the conviction based on counsel's failure to include the components of the victimization defense strategy within his original defense. This decision establishes, as a matter of law, that the defense should include these elements of the defense strategy in any self-defense case of a battered woman.

This case is just one indication of the success of the defense strategy when used in this context. In many cases, an appellate court has reversed and remanded a case because the trial court excluded a key component of the victimization defense strategy offered by defense counsel.[69] The element of the defense strategy that has most often served as the basis for appellate reversal when excluded at trial is expert testimony on the effects of abuse, usually in the form of battered woman syndrome. A further indication of the success of the defense strategy, then, is the degree of acceptance of testimony on battered woman syndrome by appellate courts.[70] According to D'Emilio (1985), expert testimony on battered woman syndrome had been accepted in nine of the fourteen jurisdictions in which it was offered by 1985. As of 1992, thirty-one states and the District of Columbia allowed expert testimony on battered woman syndrome.[71] In addition to case law, by 1992 seven states had passed statutes pertaining to the admissibility of battered woman syndrome (and, in some cases, the effects of prior violence on a defendant), and Congress had passed a resolution stating that "expert testimony concerning the nature and effect of domestic violence, including descriptions of the experiences of battered women, should be admissible when offered in a state court by a defendant in a criminal case" (reported in Lefcourt 1995:18.46).

Yet another measure of the acceptance of the victimization defense strategy within this context is the number of law review articles written about the battered woman's self-defense strategy. Between the late 1970s and 1995, approximately seventy-three law review articles about this strategy were published.[72] Although not all of these reviews favor the acceptance of the strategy, many do. However, the fact that lawyers and scholars continue to debate the validity of this strategy twenty-five years after it was initially developed and proposed only provides further evidence of its acceptance within the legal community. In fact, one could argue that this has become the primary argument pursued in such cases, the first defense strategy examined by attorneys faced with a battered woman's self-defense case.

Unlike the two uses of it discussed earlier, the use of the victimization defense strategy in battered women's self-defense cases achieved a high degree of success and acceptance. As a result, the victimization defense strategy "emerged [as] an independent argument never officially endorsed: A history of abuse could actually justify homicide" (Fletcher 1995:137). Thus, the connection between social victimization and the alleviation of responsibility was first made in these battered women's cases. The successful use of the strategy in these cases established that past social victimization could explain and justify present misconduct. Because of their past experience of abuse, these women killed in self-defense. Therefore, their actions were justified, and they were not held morally responsible. These women were victims, not culpable offenders.

Interestingly, however, this same basic strategy, though successful for battered women, was a failure in the other two types of cases. Why? Why was the strategy accepted in the context of battered women's cases but not in the context of rotten social background or brainwashing cases? This is the primary question addressed in chapter 4.

4

Extralegal Factors and the Success of the Battered Woman's Self-Defense Strategy

The victimization defense strategy was used successfully in battered women's self-defense cases although it was not accepted in the rotten social background and brainwashing cases. Why? How can this difference in outcomes be explained? In this case, to best understand changes taking place inside the courtroom, one must understand the swirl of activity surrounding the battered woman's self-defense strategy outside the courtroom. In other words, the primary factors that explain the eventual success of battered woman's self-defense are, in fact, extralegal—forces impinging on the law from the outside (see Macaulay et al. 1995:8). The other two defense arguments did not enjoy the same level of support outside the court, and therefore did not achieve the same degree of success inside the court. The sociological framework I develop here explains why the same strategy differed in its effectiveness and success in these three different types of cases.

Researchers in the sociology of law have long noted that extralegal factors influence the processes by which laws are changed and created (Hagan 1980; Vago 1994): studies in this area recognize the extent to which lawmaking on all levels— legislative, judicial, and administrative—is a social process (Macaulay et al. 1995; Tomasic 1985). Sociologists have examined a variety of factors that are instrumental in this process: interest group support (Chambliss 1964; Gusfield 1986; Hall 1952; Lindesmith 1965; Luker 1984); the work of moral entrepreneurs and elite reformers (Becker 1963; Hollinger and Lanza-Kaduce 1990; Platt 1977; Pleck 1987; Weitzman 1985); media exposure (Hollinger and Lanza-Kaduce 1990; Sutherland 1950; Tierney 1982); organizational resources (Gusfield 1986; McCarthy and Zald 1987; Pleck 1987); and social context (Hagan 1980; Pleck 1987; Sutherland 1950). While most of these analyses focus on the creation of new laws, I found that many of these same factors were influential in the institutionalization of this new legal strategy.

The three extralegal factors that account for the success of the battered woman's self-defense strategy can best be summarized as "reformers, resources, and social context." This strategy, unlike the RSB and brainwashing approaches, benefitted from the extensive and concentrated work and advocacy of a group of elite reformers. In this particular case, a small group of influential feminist lawyers and social scientists developed this new self-defense approach to correct what they perceived to be gender inequity in the formulation and application of traditional self-defense law. The work of these feminist reformers was essential because it both formulated a clear theoretical framework for understanding the use of the strategy in cases in which battered women had killed their abusers and provided specific materials to other practitioners to aid in the implementation of the strategy. They increased the accessibility of the strategy by leading seminars and classes for lawyers and social scientists on its proper application. Because of these efforts, lawyers, judges, and other legal professionals were familiarized with a viable new argument for handling such cases.

Several of these reformers founded the Women's Self-Defense Law Project, a formal organization that provided personnel, resources, and facilities specifically intended to promote and fund the use of the strategy in battered women's cases. Finally, all of this activity took place within a social landscape in which the primary tenets of the women's movement were not only familiar but were actually being institutionalized throughout society in the economy, political structure, family, and law. In fact, one could argue that the interest and attention (both public and private) generated by the women's movement made the advocacy of these elite reformers possible.

In developing the battered woman's self-defense strategy, reformers drew heavily on themes that were part of this larger movement—themes of gender equality, sex-role stereotyping, and victimization (themes repeated in the civil rights movement and therapeutic culture of the period as well). Thus, the importance of social context to the success of the strategy cannot be overlooked. The reformers used their resources and organizational base to develop a new defense approach that was consistent with and reliant on larger cultural themes available at the time.

No such advocacy or organizational support for the victimization defense strategy materialized for either the RSB cases or the brainwashing cases. And neither of these contexts saw advocates succeed in connecting the themes of the strategy to larger social concerns. Thus, the convergence of these three factors in support of the use of the victimization defense strategy on behalf of battered women explains the differential success of the approach in these three types of cases.

This is not, however, a simple one-way process of institutionalization in which feminist scholars draw on cultural tenets to develop new legal approaches that link the concepts of victimization and responsibility. The process of change also moves in the other direction. As the advocates press their claim, the approach becomes more familiar to and accepted by increasing numbers of judges, lawyers, jurors, and citizens, thereby increasing the use of victimization as an excuse from responsibility in the culture at large. As such, the success of the victimization defense strategy in this context both draws from and contributes to the larger culture of victimization.

Feminist Reformers

The battered woman's self-defense strategy was developed by a group of feminist lawyers and social scientists interested in achieving gender equality in the application of self-defense law. In the mid-1970s, before this group of advocates became interested in this area of law, "There was no such area of the law as women's self-defense" (Schneider 1986b:191). The main thrust of the reformers' argument was that self-defense was unequally applied to men and women because traditional self-defense law was based on a male model of behavior. By devising this new approach, they hoped to promote change in the way self-defense was applied to women, especially battered women who killed their abusers, and to expand the law if necessary. The activities of these advocates included lecturing, writing articles, defending battered women in court, providing consultation services to other lawyers, holding education and training sessions for lawyers and social scientists on how to handle battered women's self-defense cases, and teaching law school classes on the subject (Bochnak 1981a).

Many studies of law reform have recognized the importance of individual reformers to the successful enactment of legal change. Howard Becker's analysis of the role of "moral entrepreneurs" in the creation of marijuana laws still stands as the classic statement on the influence of reformers on the law-making process. In his words, "Someone must call the public's attention to these matters, supply the push necessary to get things done, and direct such energies as are aroused in the proper direction to get a rule created" (1963:162). This same principle applies to strategy creation and implementation.

Following in Becker's tradition, others have pointed out the extent to which professionals and social elites work for legal reform. Anthony Platt's (1977) "child-savers" were primarily social elites and moral entrepreneurs, while professional elites were more influential in the creation of computer crime laws (Hollinger and Lanza-Kaduce 1990) and in the revision of rape and abortion laws (Luker 1984; Pleck 1987) and divorce laws (Weitzman 1985).

Advocates for the reform of self-defense law were primarily professional elites—lawyers, legal scholars, and social scientists. The work of two of these elite entrepreneurs—Elizabeth Schneider and Lenore Walker—exemplifies the types of activities in which these individuals engaged in their campaign for changes in the application of self-defense law.

Elizabeth Schneider

A prominent scholar in feminist jurisprudence, Elizabeth Schneider played a primary role in the development of the battered woman's self-defense strategy. From 1973 to 1980, she worked as a staff attorney at the Center for Constitutional Rights[1] (CCR) and later as a staff attorney, and eventual Director, at the Constitutional Litigation Clinic at Rutgers Law School-Newark (Schneider 1986b). She is currently Professor of Law at Brooklyn Law School.

While on staff at CCR, Schneider began working with the Women's Self-Defense Law Project, where she helped develop the legal theory upon which the battered woman's self-defense strategy was based. In cooperation with Susan Jordan, she wrote one of the first and most influential law review articles to outline the sex bias in self-defense law and its deficiency when applied to battered women who kill their abusers (Schneider and Jordan 1978). This article fueled interest in battered women's self-defense cases and served as an impetus for the organization of the Women's Self-Defense Law Project.[2] In the years since, Schneider has written many other law articles on the use of the battered woman's self-defense strategy.

Schneider also served as co-counsel in *State v Wanrow*,[3] the landmark case that recognized the inadequacy of the "reasonable man" standard in cases involving women, in essence creating a new "reasonable woman" or "reasonable person" standard. In 1984, she continued her advocacy on behalf of battered women by serving as co-counsel to the *amicus* brief for *State v Kelly*,[4] an important battered woman's self-defense case. Here she argued for the admissibility of expert testimony on battered woman syndrome. The court found in the defendant's favor and admitted the testimony, establishing a notable precedent on the relevance and reliability of expert testimony on battered woman syndrome in such cases.

Schneider has remained active in a variety ways in promoting equality for women under the law and continues to address the legal challenges faced by battered women who kill their abusers and attempt to claim self-defense.

Lenore Walker

A feminist psychologist who began studying the effects of battering on women in 1975 (Walker 1979), Lenore Walker defines herself as an advocate and reformer fighting in all areas of society for changes in the treatment of battered women (Walker 1989:11). She is widely known for having developed a profile of the "typical" battering relationship and originating the term "battered woman syndrome" (Walker 1979, 1984). As discussed earlier, expert testimony on battered woman syndrome has become a central component of the battered woman's self-defense strategy, and the syndrome was recognized by the *DSM-III-R* (the revised third edition of the American Psychological Association's *Diagnostic and Statistical Manual of Mental Disorders*, 1987) as a subcategory of Post-Traumatic Stress Disorder (Walker 1993).

Before writing her 1979 book *The Battered Woman*, Walker had already testified in several battered women's self-defense cases on behalf of the defendant to explain how the battered woman could have reasonably perceived herself to be in imminent danger of serious bodily harm. By 1989, Walker had testified about battered woman syndrome or served in some way on behalf of the defendant in more than 150 murder trials. By 1993, Walker had taken part in over 300 cases, mainly self-defense cases (Walker 1989, 1993).

In addition to her advocacy in the courtroom, Walker has written three influential and controversial books about battered women. While the first two books, *The Battered Woman* (1979) and *The Battered Woman Syndrome* (1984), focused primarily on explaining the battered woman syndrome, they did discuss the legal problems faced by battered women who kill and the need for an adequate self-defense strategy. The third book, *Terrifying Love* (1989), dealt specifically with the legal challenges encountered by battered women who kill their abusers. In this book Walker also described her experiences as an expert witness in self-defense trials. In addition to these books, she has authored or coauthored several articles on the subject.

Walker advocates for changes in the treatment of battered women in the courtroom in other ways as well. She has organized seminars to educate lawyers and social scientists on the use of battered woman syndrome testimony in battered women's self-defense cases (Walker 1989). She has also given lectures on the subject and made occasional television appearances as an expert about such issues. As one of the most influential figures in the development and implementation of this defense strategy, she has done a great deal to educate the public in general about the problems faced by battered women and battered women who kill.

The Accessibility of the Strategy

This brief review of the work of these two central figures demonstrates that advocacy by feminist reformers in many ways made the battered woman's self-defense strategy more accessible and contributed to its eventual success.[5] The advocates ran seminars to educate other lawyers and social scientists about the use of the strategy; they provided materials to others working on similar cases; they provided information to the media on cases being tried; they assisted lawyers on cases free of charge; and they wrote a book, *Women's Self-Defense Cases* (Bochnak 1981a), that provided comprehensive information on the application of the strategy at a low cost (Bochnak 1981a). Through these diverse and sustained initiatives, the reformers established the strategy as a new and viable method of argument that could be used in cases in which battered women had killed their abusers. Because more lawyers, social scientists, and judges were familiar with the strategy, legal advocates had an additional argument available when confronted with similar cases. Thus, the reformers contributed to the acceptance of the strategy by making it more accessible to the practitioners handling such cases.

Aside from these efforts to educate others about the theoretical framework of the strategy and, in effect, to promote its use throughout the legal community, the reformers also contributed to the accessibility of the strategy by providing specific and practical materials to those who wanted to use it, in written materials and training sessions. For example, the Appendix in *Women's Self-Defense Cases* (Bochnak 1981a) provides a variety of specific materials designed to aid in the implementation of the strategy—sample jury instructions, legal memoranda, and questions to ask during the *voir dire*. Dissemination of these materials became a primary goal of the Women's Self-Defense Law Project as well (Bochnak 1981a).

Feminist advocates, then, played a significant part in establishing the successful use of the victimization defense strategy within battered women's self-defense cases. They worked to develop specific tools and methods for using the strategy and attempted to make these materials and information widely available to other legal professionals as well as the media.

The victimization defense strategy did not enjoy such widespread advocacy in the RSB and brainwashing cases. While one or two individuals pledged their support to the development of the strategy in these two types of cases, their advocacy was limited and, for the most part, short-lived. Aside from the publication of a few law review articles and lectures at legal symposia, these advocates did not do as much to ensure the widespread circulation of their ideas. In contrast, supporters of the battered woman's self-defense strategy initiated a variety of concentrated individual efforts to gain recognition for their approach. And they also formed an organization and garnered resources from outsiders to fund their activities, allowing them to expand the number and breadth of their efforts. While the work of these advocates is significant, then, their achievements would not have been possible without the organizational support of the Women's Self-Defense Law Project.

Organizational Resources: The Women's Self-Defense Law Project

Established in 1978, this organization was cosponsored by the Center for Constitutional Rights (CCR) and the National Jury Project (NJP).[6] The Project was formed "to assist lawyers around the country to more effectively represent women victims of violence who defend themselves" (Schneider 1986b). Although attorneys at the two sponsoring organizations had worked to some extent on battered women's self-defense cases before the formation of the Project in 1978, the establishment of this organization enabled lawyers and social scientists to synthesize and formalize techniques and approaches to handling such cases, as well as assist others in using the strategy.[7]

Research on legal change has established clearly the significant role of formal organizations in helping interest groups achieve desired goals. Gusfield's (1986) study of the temperance movement indicates the influence of organizations such as the Connecticut Society for the Reformation of Morals, the American Temperance Society, and the Women's Christian Temperance Union in the creation of prohibition laws. Others have detailed the role of the Federal Bureau of Narcotics in the creation and enforcement of new federal drug laws (Lindesmith 1965) and the influence of the American Medical Association and Society for Humane Abortions on abortion law reform (Luker 1984).

In addition, resource mobilization theorists have long recognized the role of formal organizations and the aggregation of resources in the success of a social movement (Gamson 1987; McCarthy and Zald 1987). Considering that legal reform is often a stated goal of social movements (Freeman 1977; Greenberg 1994; Vago 1994), this approach emphasizes how the mobilization of resources—money, personnel, facilities, and networks—in conjunction with the backing of a formal organizational structure can facilitate the achievement of such goals (Freeman 1977; McCarthy and Zald 1987).

In the case of the Women's Self-Defense Law Project, the establishment of a formal organization allowed reformers to bring together a variety of advocates familiar with such cases in one arena, allowed for the coordination of activities, and provided a resource base for these activities. The Project used the facilities of the Center for Constitutional Rights and staff members from both the CCR and the NJP (approximately fifteen staff members).[8] Though these resources were available for only two years, the Project received outside support from a variety of foundations and church agencies, ranging from The Playboy Foundation to the Board of Global Ministries of the United

Methodist Church.[9] The facilities and funding donated to the Project provided resources to support such activities as training sessions on the use of the strategy; assistance in locating expert witnesses; legal consultation on case development, jury selection, and defendant preparation; and the preparation of educational materials and attorney questionnaires (Bochnak 1981a; Schneider 1986c). These resources also supported the publication of *Women's Self-Defense Cases* (Bochnak 1981a: xvii–xviii), which outlines the use of the victimization defense strategy within battered woman's self-defense cases and "represents the accumulated insights, analyses, strategies and ideas developed by the Women's Self-Defense Law Project."

The battered woman's self-defense strategy, then, was backed by the resources of a formal organization specifically designed to support the development, formalization, and publication of the use of the strategy. No evidence is available to indicate that the use of the victimization defense strategy within the other two types of cases received such extensive organizational support. No organization developed specifically to fund the use of the strategy in all rotten social background or brainwashing cases. For example, while the NAACP did support efforts in other areas of the criminal justice system, such as capital punishment law reform, jury selection, prisoners' rights, and bail rights, no evidence indicates that the NAACP gave organizational support to the development and implementation of strategies used in rotten social background cases or black rage cases.[10]

The organizational support of the Women's Self-Defense Law Project, as well as the two cosponsoring organizations, had a significant influence on the successful use of the strategy. In many ways, the activities supported by the Project contributed to the accessibility of the strategy. The money, facilities, and personnel provided by the Project funded training sessions, case consultations, attorney questionnaires, and the production and distribution of materials about the strategy. The Project provided a mechanism and structure whereby the strategy could "reach" people in an organized, systematic manner, which could only contribute to a clearer understanding and more effective application of the approach by others. As with the efforts by feminist reformers (who to a large extent were connected to the formation of this organization), attempts to increase familiarity with the strategy, both within the legal community and among the general public, encouraged lawyers to use it and created a better understanding of such arguments by judges and potential jurors.

All of this activity, of course, did not take place in a social vacuum, but within a specific social context—an atmosphere permeated by discussions of inequality, bias, and victimization. In developing the strategy, the feminist reformers drew heavily on these cultural themes. While new and different, their approach incorporated ideas not wholly unfamiliar to judges, attorneys, and jurors. In their efforts to affect legal change in accordance with these larger cultural themes, the reformers were much like advocates attempting to promote similar changes in other social institutions, such as the family, economy, and politics. Social context, then, also played a critical role in the success of the battered woman's self-defense strategy.

Social Context and Cultural Themes

In a review of studies that examined factors influential in the lawmaking process, Hagan (1980) noted the significant impact of social context on successful law reform. For example, in his analysis of sexual psychopath laws, Sutherland (1950) argued that the creation of such laws was successful partly because they were in concert with broader social beliefs about the proper treatment of offenders. In her study of changes in spouse abuse laws, Pleck (1987) pointed to the importance of the feminist and antirape movements in establishing a social context in which spouse abuse could be addressed. Schudson (1989) refers to this as "resonance"—the extent to which an idea makes sense or is embedded within a given social context. He argues that ideas must "resonate" with an audience to be successful: ideas must be "relevant to and resonant with the life of the audience" (Schudson 1989:167; see also Corse 1996).

Therefore, in addition to the work of the feminist reformers and the organizational support of the Women's Self-Defense Law Project, it is crucial to recognize the social context in which all of this activity was taking place. After all, lawyers, judges, and jurors all exist within the same culture and draw on many of the same cultural resources when deciding, in a court of law, whether a defense strategy makes sense to them.

In their formulation of the battered woman's self-defense approach, the reformers incorporated several themes that were being articulated in the broader culture at the time. Concern over inequality and victimization were part and parcel of the civil rights movement, therapeutic movement, youth movement, and women's movement that were dominating public and private discussions during this period. And, of course, these are the focal points of the strategy—ensuring the equal treatment of women under the law and recognizing the impact of victimization on perceptions and behavior. Given their primary concern with women's inequality and victimization, however, the reformers drew on these themes as they were particularly framed by the women's movement. Relying on this particular context, then, the three specific themes sounded by the battered woman's self-defense strategy are: (1) gender equality in the law; (2) the eradication of sex-role stereotyping and bias; and (3) the recognition of female victimization and its effect on behavior.

In general, these themes reflect a cultural change in understandings of womanhood and women's place in the family and society—a change best summarized as a redefinition of womanhood away from the "woman as wife-companion" ideal and toward the "woman as person" ideal (Rothman 1978). As such, the efforts of these feminist advocates can also be understood more broadly as an attempt to change law in accordance with this new definition, an effort being replicated by others in every major social institution at the time. In other words, by using these themes as the foundation for the new approach, the reformers construct a particular view of women—women as equal to men, women as rational actors, women whose unique (and previously misunderstood and unrecognized) experiences of social victimization shape their behaviors. In addition, this redefinition of womanhood, of "woman as person," was gaining currency throughout society as most major institutions began to change in accordance with it. An understanding of social context, then, is essential to a complete understanding of the success of this version of the victimization defense strategy.

Themes of Law Reform

The use of the victimization defense strategy in battered women's self-defense cases was intended as a critique and correction of the manner in which self-defense law had traditionally been applied (see Gillespie 1989; Schneider 1980; and Schneider and Jordan 1981 for summaries of this argument). Advocates argued that traditional self-defense law was founded on a male model of behavior. Historically, they contended, self-defense law developed to apply to situations in which men, not women, commonly found themselves, such as sudden attacks by strangers and barroom brawls. Concepts crucial to self-defense, such as "imminent danger" and "proportional force," assumed that the two participants in the encounter were men of approximately equal size and strength trained in the same basic skills of self-protection. Based on such assumptions, a victim would not be in "imminent danger" unless the offender used a weapon, and would not need to use a weapon in self-defense if the offender was only using his fists. Such gender-based assumptions about the nature of self-defense situations also shaped the application of the central concept of "reasonableness" and the circumstances under which a man would reasonably perceive himself to be in imminent danger and, therefore, able to respond with proportional force.

Such a traditional construction of self-defense law does not consider that women generally defend themselves in situations quite different from this. In most self-defense situations involving women, the attacker is known by the victim—a family member or acquaintance—and the attacker is usually larger and stronger. Women are less likely to be trained in the skills necessary for adequate self-protection and can be seriously injured or even killed by a male attacker who uses no weapon other than his fists.

The feminist reformers argued that traditional self-defense law did not take the woman's situation into consideration, making self-defense less available to women than to men. As a result, they advocated for a number of changes that would more fully recognize the experiences and perspectives of women, including reformulations of the pivotal concepts of "imminent danger," "proportional force," and "reasonableness." The use of the victimization defense strategy in these cases was one way to achieve such equality by highlighting the male bias in the law and requiring the court to consider the woman's actions from her own perspective. Thus, one of the primary themes sounded by those advocating the use of the battered woman's self-defense strategy was to achieve gender equality under the law and "equalize treatment of women in the courts" (Schneider 1986c:197).

The second theme of the approach was the intention to overcome sex bias and sex-role stereotyping in the application of self-defense law (Schneider 1986a, 1986c). As Schneider and Jordan argued:

The traditional view of women who commit violent crimes is that their action was irrational or insane. Consequently, an impaired mental state defense has often been relied on automatically. We start from the premise that a woman who kills is no more "out of her mind" than a man who kills. Our work has shown that the circumstances which require a woman to commit homicide in these cases can demonstrate that her act was reasonable and necessary. (1981:5)

Because the traditional application of self-defense law did not take into consideration the woman's perspective or experience, women's actions were more likely to be defined as unreasonable, hysterical, and out of control (Rosen 1986; Schneider 1980; Schneider and Jordan 1981).

The advocates, however, claimed that if the law did consider the woman's perspective, her response to a threatening situation could be understood as a reasonable one. As the appellate court remarked in the landmark Wanrow decision, "The respondent was entitled to have the jury consider her actions in the light of her own perceptions of the situation."[11] The court went on to state that it was, in fact, *unreasonable* to assume that "a 5'4" woman with a cast on her leg and using a crutch must, under the law, somehow repel an assault by a 6'2" intoxicated man without employing weapons in her defense," indicating that when viewed from *her* perspective her actions were a reasonable response to the situation.[12]

The reformers hailed this as a significant decision supporting their definition of women as rational, controlled people who make reasonable and *justified* responses in threatening situations. They viewed this as an important step toward eradicating stereotypical views of women, especially violent women, as hysterical and even insane. To the extent that it forces judges and juries to examine the reasonableness of a woman's conduct from *her* perspective, the battered woman's

self-defense strategy becomes another tool in the effort to elim-
inate such sex-role stereotyping in the law.

Finally, this approach recognized and emphasized the extent to which these women were victims rather than
offenders—victims of abusive men and relationships, and of a
society that neglected their predicament and failed to provide
helpful resources. The victimization defense strategy, in any
context, is an attempt to explain the defendant's actions by focusing on past victimization experiences. Within the context
of battered women who kill, the strategy was designed to identify the woman as the victim of abuse and explain how this status shaped her perceptions of the threatening situation,
accounting for her murderous actions. Thus, victimization was
a third important theme of the strategy.

Schneider admits that emphasizing a woman's victimization while maintaining that her actions are reasonable and rational can be difficult (Schneider 1986c). Victimization is often
associated with passivity and helplessness, not action, reason,
and control. In many cases, placing equal emphasis on these two
themes has been a difficult balance to strike. Often when the
strategy is used, lawyers and judges choose to overemphasize
the theme of victimization and neglect the issue of rationality
and control (Schneider 1986c). Such an overemphasis paints a
portrait of female incapacity, a woman who is dazed and con-
fused and certainly unable to respond in a reasonable fashion.
This interpretation of the strategy focuses on the very stereotypes reformers want to eradicate. The portrait of the reasonable woman who actively chooses a rational course of action
given her situation is lost.[13] However, Schneider maintains that
both themes can coexist and be of equal importance in the strategy: "The woman's experience as a battered woman and her inability to leave the relationship—her victimization—is the
context in which [the reasonable] action occurs" (1986c:199).

These, then, are the three themes central to the battered

woman's self-defense strategy: (1) the emphasis on law reform to achieve equality for women in the law; (2) the focus on the eradication of sex-role stereotypes in the law; and (3) the recognition of the victimized status of the defendants. By emphasizing these central themes, the battered woman's self-defense strategy provides a reformulation of the traditional view of women in self-defense law. The stereotypical view of the irrational, hysterical wife is replaced by the rational and responsible woman who is equal to men and therefore deserving of equal treatment under the law. However, the reformers also recognized that women are not always treated as equals by society or within their own relationships, but instead are sometimes victimized and dismissed. In sum, the use of the victimization defense strategy in this particular context validated the female point of view and offered a new definition of womanhood, a definition at the forefront of public activity and debate.

The Redefinition of Womanhood

From the mid-1960s to the early 1980s, the time frame in which the battered woman's self-defense strategy took shape, the women's movement was profoundly influencing and reformulating the way Americans thought about women—as individuals, as members of a society, and as participants in relationships with men (Hole and Levine 1971, 1989; Rothman 1978; Ryan 1992). In many ways, this was a period marked by redefinition.

In *Woman's Proper Place* (1978), historian Sheila Rothman notes that the definition of womanhood—the cultural understanding of what it means to be a woman—changed significantly in the century between 1880 and 1980. In the period prior to the 1960s, the definition of "woman as wife-companion" predominated. According to this model, the role of "woman" was to take care of the home, maintain a stimulating and romantic relationship with her husband, and be a good mother (Kessler-Harris 1982; Rothman 1978). In her best-selling book of the same title, Betty Friedan (1963) labeled this definition the "feminine mystique." The feminine mystique required a woman to find fulfillment in her biological function as wife and mother and maintain a quiet dependence on her spouse, which included a quiet acceptance of violence inflicted on her in the home (Friedan 1963; Studer 1984). The definition of womanhood as "wife-companion" placed a premium on finding fulfillment through helping others reach their goals (Rothman 1978).

Additionally, the "wife-companion" model was characterized by a marital relationship in which the roles of the spouses were sharply divided: her place was in the home, his in the workplace; her energy was focused on their relationship, his on the world outside their relationship. The wife's primary obligations were "the preservation of beauty under the penalty of marital insecurity, the rendering of ego and libido satisfaction to the husband, the cultivation of social contacts advantageous to him, the maintenance of intellectual alertness, the responsibility for exorcising the demon of boredom" (Kirkpatrick, quoted in Rothman 1978:180).

Indicative of its dominance during this period, this ideal was supported by social policies and incorporated into many social institutions (Friedan 1963; Hole and Levine 1971). The criminal justice system maintained a "hands off" approach to violence in the home, reinforcing the husband's right to control family members as he saw fit (Pleck 1987). Protective legislation and a segregated labor market maintained male dominance in the work force. Women's education focused on "women's concerns" such as gardening, child development, and cooking. And sociologists and psychologists explained to America how the sex-role division of labor was biologically determined and a functional imperative (see for example Parsons and Bales 1955).

However, during the 1960s a new definition of womanhood

began to emerge—"woman as person" (Rothman 1978). This new ideal characterized women as "autonomous, energetic, and competent" and "fully capable of defining and acting in [their] own best interest[s]" (Rothman 1978:231). The role of wife and mother was no longer the defining feature of a woman's life, but only one path among many that she could choose to travel. This new definition dictated a new understanding of the relationships between men and women as well. Relationships were to be equal partnerships between two autonomous and equal people (Rothman 1978). The responsibilities of those in relationships were to be determined not by gender stereotypes but by individual preferences. Both in relationships and in society in general, the "woman as person" demanded that she be treated equally according to her abilities, not unequally because of her gender.

As noted earlier, the "woman as person" definition encapsulated the three themes emphasized by the battered woman's self-defense approach. This new model was predicated on the belief that men and women were equal and should be treated equally in all areas of society. It also attacked the traditional sex-role stereotypes of "woman is irrational, man is rational." Instead, the new definition asserted that "woman is person" just as man is; both are capable of rationality and passivity. Finally, the "woman as person" is a woman who is not a subordinate or a dependent in her relationships with men but an equal partner. However, the assertion of equality as the norm for relationships served to highlight the extent to which many women were not equal partners but instead victims of abuse and mistreatment. Thus the recognition of "woman as victim" was made possible by the new definition of "woman as person."

Gradually, this new definition of womanhood became a part of our culture. Many, if not most, women's rights groups in some way espoused the "woman as person" definition as part of their platform of beliefs.[14] For example, the original Statement of Purpose of the National Organization for Women (NOW) declared, "The time has come to confront with concrete action, the conditions which now prevent women from enjoying the equality of opportunity and freedom of choice which is their right as individual Americans, and as human beings" (quoted in Rothman 1978:235). NOW's statement about the relationships between men and women asserted that "a true partnership between the sexes demands a different concept of marriage, an equitable sharing of the responsibilities of home and children and of the economic burdens of their support" (quoted in Rothman 1978:236). These public pronouncements serve as just one indication of attempts to promote the new "woman as person" definition of womanhood.

The media also began to focus on and even embrace the "woman as person." For example, TV shows revolving around the single, working woman proliferated. *The Mary Tyler Moore Show, Julia, That Girl,* and *Police Woman* were popular television hits of the period (Press 1991).

In addition, several popular women's magazines, such as *McCall's* (July 1970) and *Ladies' Home Journal* (August 1970), ran special stories on the "women's liberation movement" in which activists explained their efforts to increase individual choice and equality for women. Widely circulated magazines such as *Time* and *Newsweek* ran cover stories on the women's movement (in their August and March 1970 editions respectively). The reporter(s) in the *Newsweek* cover story began the article by providing the following definition of the women's movement: "Talking about changes in social attitudes and customs that will allow every female to function as a separate and equal person" (*Newsweek* 1970:71). In the spring of 1972, *Ms.* magazine was launched, becoming one of the most active magazines in reporting on and supporting women's rights causes. The subscription form in the first edition states, "*Ms.* is written for all women, everywhere, in every occupation and profession . . . women who are wives, mothers, and grandmothers, or none of these—women who want to be fully a female person and proud of it" (*Ms.* 1972:113).

In addition to its usual coverage of feminist activities, *Ms.* ran stories on spouse abuse during the 1970s (August 1976, April 1977, and October 1979). Newspapers around the country also began to focus on domestic violence (Schneider and Jordan 1981). In 1977, the trial of Francine Hughes for the murder of her ex-husband (detailed in the book and film *The Burning Bed*) received wide media coverage and focused public attention on the incidence and consequences of domestic violence (McNulty 1980). In addition, many feminist groups (especially groups involved in the women's liberation branch of the movement) focused on the victimization of women in society and in relationships, prompting changes in the criminal justice system. Advocates highlighted the extent to which women were victims of rape, sexual harassment, battery, pornography, and an unjust criminal justice system that ignored all of these issues (Ryan 1992). In many ways, then, feminist reformers drew on themes available in the social landscape and, in developing their new defense approach, attempted to reshape the law in accordance with the new definition of womanhood. Of course, the law was not the only institution undergoing such a change.

Gradually other social institutions began to accommodate this new definition as advocates lobbied for change. Over time, changes were implemented in hiring policies and pay structures in the labor force, educational materials in the schools and churches, and assistance programs for working mothers, such as day care and work training (Freeman 1975; Hole and Levine 1971; Rothman 1978). Within the private sphere, advocates attacked the sex-role division of labor within the family, advocated for abortion law reform, and fought laws and customs requiring women to take their husbands' names (Hole and Levine 1971; Luker 1984; Rothman 1978). They fought too for the enforcement of spouse abuse laws that emphasized the extent to which women were often victims within their own homes, and attempted to revoke the age-old male privilege allowing men to beat their wives. A brief review of the changes in four primary social institutions—the family, the economy, education, and politics—to recognize the new woman can illuminate the gradual cultural adjustment to this new ideal.

Family. Perhaps more than any other institution, the family was impacted by the new definition of womanhood. Because the old definition of woman as "wife-companion" was so central to the operation of the family, changes in that definition greatly affected the family unit, especially the relationships between husbands and wives. For example, before the 1970s, custom dictated that a woman assume her husband's name upon marriage, symbolizing the merging of two people into one identity, the one being the husband as head of the household (Hole and Levine 1971; Weitzman 1981). During the 1970s, women began to protest this tradition, arguing that changing one's name constituted a loss of personal identity. As a full and equal partner in the marital relationship, they argued, women should be allowed to keep their given names if they so chose. In 1975, Hawaii's statute requiring a woman to take her husband's name was declared unconstitutional (Krause 1995).

The 1970s also saw significant changes in divorce laws, changes that supported the new definition of womanhood as well as the new definition of relationships between men and women. Traditional fault-based divorce laws were founded on gendered understandings of marriage (Weitzman 1985). Upon divorce, men and women were punished and rewarded according to whether they adhered to the gender-based obligations of each. However, no-fault divorce laws, first initiated in California in 1970, aimed to treat husbands and wives as equal participants in the marriage and assumed that women had the same ability to become self-sufficient after divorce as men. As Weitzman states (1985:31–32), "the new law no longer assumes that husbands will be responsible for the financial support of their former wives. Nor does it seek to maintain the dependency of homemakers and mothers after divorce." Thus, the marital relationship was reconceptualized as a relationship between equals with the woman no longer solely defined as homemaker.

Abortion law reform too can be seen as evidence of the entrenchment of the new ideal (Hole and Levine 1971; Luker 1984; Rothman 1978). A belief in abortion on demand signals a belief that motherhood "is only one of several roles [a woman can play], a burden when defined as the only role" (Luker 1984:214). Controversy over abortion becomes, to a great extent, controversy over the definition of womanhood and the place of motherhood within that definition. A repeal of laws requiring a husband's permission for an abortion signals a redefinition of the marital relationship as one between equals, rather than one governed by the husband, and reinforces the view of women as independent people capable of making important decisions about their lives.

A final area of change within the family that supports the "woman as person" definition is the movement to define and combat domestic violence. The victimization of women within the family became a primary focus of many women's rights organizations (Pleck 1987; Tierney 1982). Throughout Western history, in their role as head of the family, men had been given the right to beat their wives (see Browne 1987 and Okun 1986 for a history of these laws). Although these laws were changed prior to the 1970s, ostensibly outlawing domestic violence, enforcement of the new laws was weak. In the mid-1970s, a submovement emerged within the women's movement that focused on the enforcement of domestic violence laws and lobbied for further legal changes to decrease women's victimization within the home: mandatory reporting laws, the enforcement of protection orders, and support for battered women's shelters (Browne 1987; Okun 1986; Tierney 1982). Gradually, such changes have been instituted.

Through these efforts, the battered women's advocates were fighting for recognition of the new definition of womanhood and of relationships between men and women. Under traditional understandings of marriage, women could not be victims of abuse because men held the legal right to beat their spouses. However, under the new definition of woman as "person," women gained the right to be free of abuse just as men are. As a result, their victimization within the family could be recognized because men no longer held the right to abuse, but instead were expected to treat their spouses as equal, competent individuals. Recognition of the victimization of women within the family signified some degree of acceptance of the new definition of womanhood.

Economy. The new ideal also required a recognition of the productivity potential of women in the work force, as well as an understanding of their competence and capabilities. Whereas the "woman as wife-companion" was primarily the guardian of the emotional realm—making a cheery home, being a good mother, maintaining an exciting marital relationship—the "woman as person" sought involvement in all areas of life, especially in the economic realm. In 1963 President Kennedy provided support for the new definition of womanhood within the economic sphere by signing the Equal Pay Act, requiring men and women to receive equal pay for equal work performed under equal conditions (Hole and Levine 1971). Although enforcement of the law was slow, gains were gradually made in many areas.

During this period, women's labor force participation also changed dramatically as more married women and married women with young children entered the work force—a further indication of the entrenchment of the new understanding of women as both mothers and workers. Early in the 1960s, few married women with young children worked outside the home. By 1980, however, one-half of wives with preschoolers and three-fifths of wives with school-age children worked outside the home (see Bianchi and Spain 1986). Not only were more wives and mothers working, but they were working more. Before the 1960s, those married women who did work usually did so only on a part-time basis and exited the labor force frequently (for example, to have children). However, during the 1960s and 1970s, these patterns changed as more married women worked full-time and maintained strong attachments to their jobs. Women also began to make inroads in a number of formerly male-dominated job sectors, such as managerial positions and technical jobs, which somewhat reduced the gender segregation in the labor force.

Many of these changes in labor force participation and legislation indicated that women, especially married women with children, were moving out of the home and into the economic realm, an area formerly reserved for and dominated by their husbands (according to the dictates of the "woman as wife-companion" model of womanhood). These changes reinforced the new definition of women as competent individuals not solely defined by their relationships with men and their role as homemakers, but instead as individuals deserving of equal treatment and opportunities outside the home as well.

Education. Similar changes occurred in education as more opportunities opened to women, especially in areas formerly defined as "male." In 1972, Congress passed Title IX of the Civil Rights Act, outlawing sex discrimination in schools receiving federal funding. Colleges and universities were forced to reevaluate their hiring and promotion procedures for female faculty, as well as their admissions standards for female students. Studies indicated that before the passage of Title IX female faculty with the same qualifications were typically paid less than their male counterparts, and female students were held to higher admissions standards (Hole and Levine 1971).

In addition to administrative changes in education, women's participation in education changed dramatically during the period. Between 1960 and 1980, the proportion of college students who were female increased from one-third to one-half (see Bianchi and Spain 1986). The number of older women going back to school, women more likely to be wives and mothers, also increased significantly. Between 1974 and 1981, the number of women thirty-five and over who enrolled in higher education rose by 72 percent. During this same period, more women received degrees in areas dominated by men than ever before. For example, between 1965 and 1980 the proportion of business degrees conferred on women rose from 8 percent to 34 percent, and in architecture the proportion rose from 8 percent to 28 percent. Between 1960 and 1980, the percentage of women graduating from medical school went from 6 percent to 23 percent, and for law school it rose from 2 percent to 30 percent.

Not only were more women breaking out of sex-role stereotypes by attending college more often and getting more degrees in male-dominated fields, feminists were engaged in a critique of the content of education itself, attacking the extent to which the education system and the materials used perpetuated earlier stereotypes of women as homemakers, as passive and dependent (see Weitzman 1979 for a summary of this critique). For example, analyses of elementary school readers and educational achievement tests revealed that males were more often portrayed as leaders possessing intelligence, creativity, and initiative. Females, on the other hand, were most commonly portrayed within the context of the home, performing domestic duties, and were more likely to be inactive and lacking in ambition and creativity (Child, Potter, and Levine 1960; Saario, Jacklin, and Tittle 1973; Women on Words & Images 1975).

Feminists also focused on the tracking systems in high schools that filtered boys into shop and girls into home economics. Again, such systems merely reinforced gender stereotypes among young people and encouraged females to develop skills in lower-paying, less-valued activities (Saario, Jacklin, and Tittle 1973; Weitzman 1979). As a result of this criticism, many schools reevaluated their classroom curricula and tracking procedures. Thus, within the institution of education the "woman as person" model was supported to some extent by the eradication of sex-role stereotypes on all levels and the enforcement of equal standards for women and men.

Politics. One of the first significant political actions to support the new definition of womanhood was the passage in 1964 of Title VII of the Civil Rights Act. This law prohibited discrimination based on race, color, religion, national origin, and *sex* by private employers, employment agencies, and unions (Freeman 1975; Hole and Levine 1971), thus establishing as federal policy that women and men were to be treated equally by employers. Enforcement of Title VII became one of the primary focuses of NOW and other women's rights organizations (Hole and Levine 1971). This legislation sent the message that women had a valid and equal place in the economy.

Another important political issue of the period, one that attracted much attention and controversy, was the debate over the establishment of a network of federally funded day care centers. Such a network would enable women to work and pursue careers, placing them on a more equal footing with men in the economic arena (Rothman 1978). The effort to establish this network was lead by Marian Wright Edelman, head of the Children's Defense Fund, and U.S. Congress members Shirley Chisholm and Walter Mondale. After much debate, the Child Development Act, which provided a program of federally supported child care facilities, was passed in 1971. However, the legislation was vetoed by President Nixon, who viewed it as an attack on the traditional "family-centered approach" to child-rearing (Rothman 1978:276).

Few issues embodied the change in the definition of womanhood like the debate over child care centers. Government support of such facilities would allow many women to pursue full-time employment by leaving some child-care responsibilities to others, and would therefore provide significant validation for the "woman as person" definition. Those opposed to the establishment of such facilities viewed it as an attack on the traditional family structure and as detrimental to America's children.

Of course, the single most important political issue in support of the new definition of womanhood was the debate over the enactment of the Equal Rights Amendment (ERA).[15] Although the ERA received favorable reactions after its initial passage by Congress in the early 1970s, the opposition solidified quickly. Feminists and other women's rights supporters argued that the ERA would elevate "a new definition of womanhood to a national norm," thereby legitimating the idea that "married women should work—that women had to find fulfillment in their own accomplishments, not in their husbands' or childrens' " (Rothman 1978:260). The ERA embodied the new understanding of women as equal, autonomous, and competent individuals. Opponents, however, defined the ERA as an attack on "the primacy of domestic roles for women" (Rothman 1978:259). The ERA issue symbolized and popularized the struggle over old and new definitions of womanhood. That a national debate on this issue was so animated is clear evidence of the changing understanding of women's "proper place."

The law, then, was not the only institution changing in accordance with the new definition of womanhood. Such change was a prominent cultural impulse of the time. The activities initiated by these feminist legal reformers were not unlike activities taking place in many areas of society. As a result, the American public (which includes lawyers, judges, and potential jurors) was familiar with the new definition of womanhood, the view of women as competent individuals deserving of equal treatment in society and in the home. Individuals were becoming more aware of the female perspective on life in America—a perspective that sees inequality, stereotyping, and victimization, as well as myths and misconceptions about their lives and needs.

In developing the battered woman's self-defense strategy, feminist reformers drew on this environment. They formulated a new approach that emphasized inequality, biased stereotypes, and victimization. They formulated an approach founded on the "woman as person" model of womanhood. By tying their strategy directly to these broader cultural themes, they made their argument more theoretically accessible. These were not ideas that were foreign to judges, jurors, and attorneys. They then launched a widespread campaign to make their new strategy not only theoretically accessible but practically accessible as well (see the previous discussion of the activities of the reformers). Social context, then, is central to understanding the success of the victimization defense strategy in battered women's self-defense cases.

Rotten Social Backgrounds and Brainwashing

What about the role of social context in RSB and brainwashing cases? The advocates who pushed for RSB and brainwashing versions of the victimization defense strategy were not as successful at connecting to and incorporating themes from the cultural environment. As a result, these approaches reached a much more limited audience because they appeared to be isolated legal arguments rather than legal versions of broad cultural impulses. Simply put, the advocates for these two approaches did not adequately frame their arguments for success.

Of the two, the RSB approach was best situated to draw from the social landscape. As a defense for poor and minority populations, advocates could have capitalized on the inequality and victimization themes that were part of the social environment (and had been made particularly relevant to these types of cases by the civil rights movement). However, the bulk of the advocacy for this approach did not take that form (with the possible exceptions of the work of David Bazelon and Paul Harris). While some did discuss the possible broad-based use of such a defense for the economically deprived, only a small cadre offered the strategy as a way to rectify racial or class inequality in the law—a way to make the system more equitable for the abused and downtrodden. In addition, advocates could not agree on the actual form such a strategy should take. Should it be an excuse or a justification defense? On this point feminist reformers never wavered: battered woman's self-defense was to be a justification strategy clearly tied to broader cultural themes. Of course, the limited advocacy and organizational support for the RSB approach only exacerbated the difficulty in making this a legal solution to more widespread problems.

One could argue that the failure of the RSB strategy is less related to these factors than it is a result of the social status of the defendants—lower-income minority males. Social status does, after all, affect the disposition of cases (Black 1976, 1989); it could easily also affect attempts to institutionalize a new strategy. In many circumstances, I find this argument persuasive, but not in this case. Why would a strategy fail when used for the poor and minorities but succeed when used for women? The statuses of both types of defendants are low; both are minority groups subject to bias and stereotyping. I am not convinced that judges and jurors would readily overcome their gender biases while clinging to their class and race biases (unless, as I suggest, it is because a full-scale effort has been initiated to help them overcome their gender biases). In fact, if social status were the determining factor, the version of the strategy with the highest probability of success would be the brainwashing case: if a wealthy white heiress cannot use this to her benefit, then status must not be an adequate explanation in this situation.[16] "Reformers, resources, and social context" provides a much more complete explanatory framework for the differential success of the strategy.

Brainwashing advocates made no attempt to connect their arguments to broader cultural issues. Theirs was primarily a legal debate about the legal legitimacy of a defense strategy that would affect a limited array of defendants (POWs, cult members, and terrorism victims). Their strategy certainly received a wealth of public attention; however, the publicity surrounding the approach was due to the identity of the defendant in one high-profile case, not the cultural resonance of the argument.

Only feminist reformers where successful in framing their strategy by linking the fundamental themes of the defense to broader and more familiar cultural concerns. By making the battered woman's self-defense strategy theoretically accessible within its social landscape, the advocates could then focus on making the approach practically accessible as well. The writing, lecturing, and teaching efforts of the reformers disseminated the strategy to a large audience. Organizational support from the Women's Self-Defense Law Project funded training sessions, case consultations, and the distribution of specific materials to aid in the application of the strategy. As a result, judges and attorneys had access to a new defense strategy in the cases of battered women who killed, and jurors were confronted with a strategy that was not culturally unfamiliar. Thus, elite reformers, organizational support, and social context are the extralegal factors that explain the successful implementation of the victimization defense strategy in battered women's self-defense cases.

Of course, as the strategy gains recognition and success, others want to use it too, both in and out of the courtroom. Outside the courtroom, the acceptability of using victimization as an excuse to responsibility increases, possibly contributing to the further growth of the culture of victimization. Inside the courtroom, more defendants want to use the approach to their benefit. As a result, the use of the victimization defense strategy expands to a variety of different types of cases.

5

Expanding the Use of the Victimization Defense Strategy

Anyone with even the slightest interest in media events over the past few years would probably recognize the names "Menendez" and "Bobbitt." Certainly, by media accounts, American criminal justice has in recent years witnessed an explosion in cases relying on the victimization defense strategy. And the Menendez brothers and Lorena Bobbitt have become the poster children for this legal trend. Some of the cases topping the news over the past five years have been: Lyle and Eric Menendez's use of a defense based on battered child syndrome to support an imperfect self-defense plea in the shooting deaths of their parents (Arenella 1993; Fletcher 1995); Lorena Bobbitt's use of the strategy based on battered woman syndrome to support a temporary insanity plea in the mutilation of her husband (*Chicago Tribune* 1994; Crawford 1994);

Colin Ferguson's initial intention to use a "black rage" defense after he killed six people on the Long Island Railroad (Mills 1994; Page 1994); serial killer Joel Rifkin's initial reliance on the strategy based on adopted child syndrome (McQuiston 1994); and Daimian Osby's use of the strategy in conjunction with urban survival syndrome testimony in the shooting deaths of two acquaintances (Hamblin 1994; Milloy 1994).

While two of these cases—the Ferguson and Rifkin cases—abandoned the strategy before trial, the remaining three cases relied on the victimization defense strategy with a degree of success. Bobbitt won an acquittal based on temporary insanity, and the first Menendez and Osby trials ended in mistrials when jurors deadlocked over appropriate verdicts.[1]

The question then becomes: Is this a real change in the law or merely a fiction of media trends? In one sense, this supposed explosion is a fiction: cases using the victimization defense strategy did not suddenly appear in court at the beginning of the 1990s. The number of battered women successfully using the approach has steadily increased since the early 1980s, while defendants in other types of cases have been able to use it to their advantage since the late 1980s. The media is, however, pointing to a real increase in the number and types of cases in which the victimization defense strategy can be used. The institutionalization of the strategy in battered women's cases as a viable, relatively successful method of argument by the defense has served as a basis for its expansion into other types of cases. As Fletcher (1995:141) argues in his discussion of the battered woman's self-defense strategy as adapted by the Menendez defense, one of the principles guiding legal thought is "the egalitarian impulse toward generalization by analogy. The courts cannot recognize a defense for the blue-eyed and refuse it to the brown-eyed. There is no way of limiting a new defense to a privileged class." Once a new strategy has been successfully institutionalized in one context, lawyers will inevitably try to adapt it to fit other contexts as well.[2]

This expansion has occurred along three primary dimensions. First, while the strategy was originally used solely in defense of women, men and children have since adapted it to fit their cases. Thus, though it began as a specific approach designed to address the legal challenges faced by battered women, lawyers have found ways to successfully argue the strategy in cases of men and children who have been similarly abused. As a result, the victimization defense strategy is now available to virtually any type of defendant.

Second, the use of the approach has expanded to include cases in which the defendant and victim are not intimates. In battered women's self-defense cases, the battered woman and her victim are or have been intimately related in some way: the victim is a husband, boyfriend, lover, or ex-husband. In fact, the strategy relies on this intimacy for its logic. The battered woman has suffered past victimization at the hands of the victim, which explains why she perceives herself to be in imminent danger when approached or threatened by him again. However, more recent applications have not required this level of intimacy between the defendant and victim. Expansion along this dimension includes cases in which the defendant and victim are mere acquaintances or even strangers. The strategy has even been accepted in cases in which the defendant is convicted of a "victimless" crime. The type of relationship between the defendant and victim, then, is another dimension of expansion.

A final dimension concerns the type of social victimization from which the defendant claims to suffer. All of the cases discussed thus far have involved physical battering: defendants claim to have been physically abused in the past, impacting their perceptions and behaviors in the present. A few more recent cases, however, have relied on more abstract and generalized types of social victimization—war trauma and social deprivation—as the basis for the defense's argument. For example, one defendant argued that growing up in a violent and deprived inner-city environment produced a psychosis that caused her to commit crimes (Flaherty 1995; Harris 1997). While this form of the strategy has not been completely rejected by the courts, it has not achieved the same level of acceptance as the first two dimensions. Continued expansion along this dimension is tenuous and limited.

The use of the victimization defense strategy, then, has proliferated. Defendants have access to the approach in a wider variety of cases using a wider variety of defenses. Apparently, judges and jurors are allowing more defendants to claim the victim status and use that status to relieve themselves of responsibility for their actions, a tendency that both draws from and contributes to the broader culture of victimization. Interestingly, however, the courts have not accepted every form of expansion. Those using the strategy based on a type of social victimization other than physical battering have had limited success. In essence, while allowing victims to join the ranks of those who can be excused from responsibility, courts seem to be limiting *who* can be legally defined as a victim to only those who have suffered physical abuse. I will return to this point after examining the dimensions of expansion in more detail.

Expansion of Defendants

As a strategy specifically designed to alleviate legal inequities in the treatment of battered women, the first successful uses of the victimization defense strategy were obviously by women. Female defendants used the strategy to their advantage throughout the early to mid-1980s. During this period, the strategy was gradually established and institutionalized as a valid defense approach in battered women's self-defense cases as appellate courts across the country accepted it as a new, viable defense argument.

Men as Defendants

In 1989 an appellate court for the first time stated its intention to allow the strategy to be used by men as well. In *Commonwealth v Stonehouse*, the court wrote, "We refer to the syndrome as the battered *woman* syndrome inasmuch as it has been described in the literature on the subject in this manner. . . . We recognize, however, that there are instances where the victims of physical, sexual and psychological abuse may be men. We shall apply the rules pertaining to the syndrome to men as well as to women."[3] Here the court indicates its willingness to accept testimony about the past abuses suffered by men at the hands of others, as well as expert psychological testimony about the effects of that abuse. In essence, the court is recognizing that men can be victims too, and therefore should be allowed to use the victimization defense strategy on their own behalf.

While the court's resolve to accept the approach when used by a man was not tested in that particular case, it was soon afterward, in the 1992 case of *Commonwealth v Kacsmar*.[4] At trial, Kacsmar was convicted of voluntary manslaughter in the shooting death of his brother. During the trial, the defendant had claimed that he acted in self-defense and had offered all elements of the victimization defense strategy in his defense, including expert psychiatric testimony that he was a victim of battered person syndrome. The testimony on battered person syndrome was excluded in the original trial, providing the basis of Kacsmar's appeal.

According to the appellate review, the defendant had testified at trial that his brother had abused him on several occasions: "Francis [the brother] continually abused him psychologically and physically for an extended period of time prior to this event."[5] In addition, the defendant had intended to introduce the testimony of Dr. K. Stanko, a psychiatrist, who would have testified that Kacsmar's fear of death at the hands of his brother "was based partially upon the history of psychological and physical abuse."[6] The court goes on to add: "Dr. Stanko would have explained the characteristics of victims of psychological and physical abuse and would have opined that appellant was the victim of psychological and physical abuse inflicted by his brother based upon certain victim characteristics demonstrated by appellant."[7] A psychologist also involved in the case even concluded that the "appellant's environment was similar to that endured by a battered wife."[8] Clearly, then, all elements of the victimization defense strategy were present in this case, and those involved recognized its similarity to the battered women's self-defense cases in which the strategy was typically offered.

The appellate court reversed the decision of the trial court, admitted the expert testimony on battered person syndrome, and remanded the case for a new trial, thereby indicating its acceptance of the use of the victimization defense strategy by a man. The court based its decision on the earlier resolution made in *Stonehouse*, writing "We find no reasoned distinction between the evidence analyzed in *Stonehouse* and the evidence which appellant sought to introduce herein."[9] Not only did the court allow the use of the strategy by a male, but the judges supported their decision by stating the similarity between this case and a battered woman's self-defense case in which the strategy was previously accepted. This case represents the first successful expansion of the use of the strategy to a male defendant.

Since this initial judicial support for the expansion of the approach to men, a number of more recent trial-level uses of the strategy by men have gained some media attention. For example, the use of the strategy by Daimian Osby, who testified that he was a victim of urban survival syndrome as a result of living in an inner-city ghetto, won him a mistrial in a murder case that many legal analysts considered "open and shut" (Hamblin 1994).

A second case that captured the media spotlight involved a

man who used the strategy to get a conviction on a lesser charge. In 1994, when Moosa Hanoukai bludgeoned his wife to death with a pipe wrench, most legal commentators viewed it as an easy murder conviction (Gregory 1994). However, Hanoukai argued at trial that he was a victim of husband battering, or "meek-mate syndrome" as one article called it (Slade 1994). He claimed that over twenty-five years of marriage, his wife had abused him physically and psychologically. Because of his Iranian-Jewish heritage, he was not allowed to escape the abuse by getting a divorce (Gregory 1994; Slade 1994), leaving him with no other alternative for escape but murder. The jury reduced his second-degree murder charge to voluntary manslaughter. Though the majority of defendants who avail themselves of this approach continue to be women, the Kacsmar decision opens the door to other defendants who find this an attractive and applicable defense argument.

Children as Defendants

Courts, then, are beginning to accept the use of the strategy by men as well as women. In addition, within the past two or three years, the courts have recognized the validity of the strategy when used by children. In 1984, *Jahnke v State*[10] became the first (though unsuccessful) case of parricide in which the defense asserted a self-defense argument based on the strategy developed in battered women's self-defense cases.

In this case, Richard Jahnke had killed his father when the father returned home from a night out. According to Jahnke, his father had been beating him, his sister, and his mother for years.[11] In his self-defense argument, Jahnke offered all elements of the victimization defense strategy in support of his plea, citing its use in battered women's self-defense cases as justification for its acceptance in this case. The court allowed the admission of all elements of the strategy except expert testimony on the psychological consequences of battering on children.

Jahnke argued that such testimony was indistinguishable from expert testimony on battered woman syndrome, and therefore should be admitted. The court disagreed, stating "We do not perceive how the offer of proof presented by the appellant was sufficient to satisfy the criteria for admissibility of expert testimony."[12] The court went on to admonish the defense for offering a defense strategy designed "to secure the recognition of a special defense in a homicide case for victims of family abuse."[13] The strategy was rejected by the court, and Jahnke's conviction was affirmed.

In the years that followed, a number of battered child self-defense cases relying on the victimization defense strategy reached the appellate level only to be rejected.[14] As indicated by the Jahnke case, the element of the strategy that proved most difficult to admit in many of these cases was expert psychological testimony about the impact of battering on a child, or testimony about battered child syndrome.[15] The first case to recognize testimony on battered child syndrome in support of a self-defense plea by a battered child was *State v Janes*, in 1993.[16] As a result, this became the first case to accept the victimization defense strategy when used by children.

In August 1988, Andrew Janes shot his stepfather Walter Jaloveckas as the latter came home from work (Monahan and Walker 1994). According to the appellate court, during the trial Andrew and others testified about a "litany of abusive behavior by Walter toward Andrew and his family" over a period of ten years.[17] The court focused extensively on Walter's behavior, recounting numerous specific instances in which Walter had beaten or punched Andrew. In its opening statement in the case, the court made clear its opinion of Andrew's status in the family: "Each of the residents of the Jaloveckas/Janes home could readily be identified as a victim."[18]

In support of Andrew's self-defense plea, a psychiatrist testified that "as a result of the chronic and enduring abuse that he received as a child and as an adolescent" and "as a product of the multiple trauma that he experienced, the multiple assaults that he experienced, the long-standing abuse that he experienced from Mr. Jaloveckas," Andrew believed himself to be in imminent danger at the time of the incident.[19] However, the trial court disallowed the testimony and rejected Janes's request that self-defense instructions be given to the jury.

On appeal, the court ruled that "battered child syndrome is admissible to help prove self-defense whenever such a defense is relevant."[20] In its justification for this ruling, the court noted the similarities between battered child syndrome and battered woman syndrome, which the court had previously ruled to be admissible: "Both syndromes find their basis in abuse-induced PTSD [post-traumatic stress disorder] and elicit a similar response from abuse victims. . . . we can see no reason to treat these two syndromes differently. Given the close relationship between the battered woman and battered child syndromes, the same reasons that justify admission of the former apply with equal force to the latter."[21] By ruling to admit the final element of the victimization defense strategy, the court explicitly recognized the validity of the strategy when used by children in parricide cases and indicated its reliance on the successful use of the strategy in battered women's self-defense cases as support for its conclusions. As a result, the court remanded the case for retrial and instructed the trial court to reconsider its decision to disallow self-defense instructions in light of the testimony on battered child syndrome and evidence of the abuse suffered by the defendant. Based on this decision, other states have begun to admit expert testimony on battered child syndrome,[22] paving the way for the further use of the victimization defense strategy on behalf of children.

Soon after this case was decided, another now infamous parricide trial took place—the trial of Eric and Lyle Menendez in the shooting deaths of their parents, Jose and Kitty. Possibly no other case has done more to publicize the expansion of the victimization defense strategy to defendants who are children.[23]

In summer 1989, Eric and Lyle shotgunned their parents to death while Jose and Kitty sat watching television. In their trial in 1993, the brothers argued that they were victims of years of physical and sexual abuse at the hands of their father and, as a result, suffered from battered child syndrome. They offered testimony about the past abuse, and expert psychological testimony about the psychological effects of that abuse on their perceptions of danger (Abrahamson 1993a, 1993b). This testimony was offered to bolster their plea of imperfect self-defense, a variation on self-defense that recognizes that the defendants' perceptions of imminent danger were real although unreasonable (Fletcher 1995).

In interviews, the brothers' lawyer, Leslie Abramson, made it clear that she intended to present a "defense for battered children that would draw on the innovations developed for battered women" (Fletcher 1995:141–142). Juries for both Eric and Lyle deadlocked, and the judge declared a mistrial, an outcome that could be considered a success given the brutality of the murders and the apparent passivity of the victims at the time they were killed. In their retrial, the defense was severely restricted by the judge in the presentation of innuendo of past alleged abuse, thus limiting the presentation of the full victimization defense strategy. This time the brothers were convicted and sentenced to life in prison. Though the brothers' defense failed the second time around, its relative success in the first trial and acceptance by the trial judge was made possible by the judicial support for the use of the strategy given by the Janes court.

Thus, the category of defendants who are able to use the victimization defense strategy has expanded to include not only men but also children. The courts have recognized the validity of the strategy and have determined that the reasoning behind the strategy applies equally well to men and children. In the years to come, expansion along this dimension will no doubt continue.

Interestingly, the Kacsmar and Janes courts explicitly re-lied on the successful use of the strategy by battered women to justify extending it to other defendants. This serves as a fur-ther indication of the acceptance of the strategy in battered women's self-defense cases, but also as a recognition that it was the battered woman's context in which the strategy was *first* successfully used.

Expansion of the Relationship between Defendant and Victim

As developed in battered women's self-defense cases, the strategy was applied to cases in which the defendant and victim were or had been sexually intimate. Women using the strategy included those who had killed their spouses, ex-spouses, common-law husbands, and boyfriends or lovers.[24] In all of these cases, the woman had killed the person who had previously abused her, a person she had once loved.

Two of the cases discussed earlier—the Kacsmar and Janes cases—indicate the courts' willingness to accept the use of the strategy in cases characterized by another form of intimacy as well—familial intimacy. Kacsmar used the strategy after killing his brother and Janes after killing his parents. In addition, some legal scholars are advocating for the further extension of the strategy to gay and lesbian relationships, yet another form of sexual intimacy (Bricker 1993; Dupps 1991). However, appel-late courts have yet to recognize its use in cases involving this type of relationship.

Aside from the intimate relationships to which the ap-proach typically applies, the victimization defense strategy has gradually been accepted in cases in which the relationship be-tween the defendant and victim is more distant. Cases in which the defendant and victim are acquaintances or even strangers have now been recognized by the courts. The strat-egy has even been used in cases of crimes like welfare fraud and drug distribution, which arguably have no identifiable victims. One way to understand the expanded use of the victimization defense strategy is on a scale of intimacy. The approach was initially used in cases characterized by a high level of intimacy and has gradually moved along the scale toward cases characterized by low intimacy.

Another interesting point about the expansion along this dimension involves the "innocence" of the victim. In other words, cases with a high level of intimacy are generally those in which the defendant killed an intimate (a husband, boyfriend, or brother) who had previously physically abused the defendant: the abused strikes back at the abuser. However, in the cases characterized by lower levels of intimacy, this is not the case: the abuser and the eventual victim are *not* the same person. Instead, the defendant claims to have been abused by an intimate sometime in the past, causing him or her to strike out at an *innocent* third party. The expansion, then, along this dimension indicates the further valid application of the strategy not only to a variety of types of relationships but also to an entirely different sort of situation. Whereas in the past critics could have argued that the strategy was only successful because it represented a form of popular justice—the victim got what he deserved for abusing the defendant—this logic no longer applies if the abuser and victim are separate individuals. Few, I think, would argue that popular justice has been served if an innocent third party dies because the defendant was beaten by someone else. As such, the expansion of the strategy to this type of case is only a further indication of its acceptance as a valid defense approach.

Acquaintance Cases

The first expansion of the use of the strategy beyond cases involving intimate relationships can be found in *State v Williams*.[25] In this case the defendant killed an innocent acquaintance. The defendant Williams had been in a five-year relationship with a married man, Louis Teague, by whom she had a daughter. At trial, Williams testified that the five-year relationship had been characterized by physical abuse, including numerous beatings, and that Teague had kicked her while she was pregnant.[26]

On the night of the homicide, the defendant met Teague at a friend's house. A fight ensued in which the defendant was beaten by Teague. She attempted to escape by fleeing to her car, but he followed. In her efforts to escape, she accidentally hit the friend, who had also followed into the parking lot. Believing the injured person to be Teague and remembering his threats to kill her if she ever hurt him, the defendant ran over the injured friend again, resulting in his death.[27]

The defendant argued during her trial that she had acted in self-defense and offered the victimization defense strategy, including expert testimony that she was a victim of battered spouse syndrome, to support her plea. The trial court ruled that testimony on battered spouse syndrome was not admissible in this case because the defendant and Teague were not married.[28] The appellate court reversed this decision and remanded the case for retrial, stating "It is clear that . . . other courts and commentators have [not] drawn any distinction between married and unmarried women as being subject to the syndrome."[29]

In admitting the expert psychological testimony on battered spouse syndrome, this court became the first to accept the use of the victimization defense strategy in a case in which the victim was not in an intimate relationship with the defendant.

In some ways, this case is similar to the battered women's cases in which the strategy was initially successful. Williams's victimization was at the hands of her lover, a characteristic common to battered women's self-defense cases. In this way the case is similar to the battered women's cases; the cause of the defendant's social victimization is physical abuse by an intimate. However, Williams's argument is fundamentally different from battered women's cases in that the defendant's social victimization is used to explain her actions toward a third party. Whereas battered women typically offer their experiences of social victimization to justify their treatment of the person responsible for that victimization (the abusive husband), Williams used her social victimization to justify her treatment of an innocent third party. While the Williams decision supports the use of the victimization defense strategy in cases in which the defendant and victim are not intimates, it also validates its use when the victim is an innocent bystander.

Stranger Cases

Not long after the Williams decision, the court accepted the use of the strategy for the first time in a case in which the defendant and the victim were strangers. Debra and Terrance Romero were convicted of second-degree robbery and four counts of attempted robbery.[30] In most of these incidents, the two defendants had picked people at random to rob while the victims were sitting in their cars.

Debra testified that she had been living with Terrance for a number of months during which time he had severely and repeatedly beaten her. According to her testimony, she had committed the robberies while under duress, fearing his abuse if she did not do as he had instructed her.[31] Debra's duress defense relied on all elements of the victimization defense strategy, except for the omission of testimony about the psychological impact of abuse on her behavior and perceptions.[32]

In her appeal, Debra Romero claimed that her trial counsel was ineffective in not providing expert psychological testimony about battered woman syndrome—in other words, in not providing a complete victimization defense strategy. Romero contended that such testimony would have explained why she did not leave Terrance and how "she entertained a good-faith objectively reasonable and honest belief that her act was necessary to prevent an imminent threat of greater harm."[33] The appellate court agreed, stating "If BWS testimony is relevant to credibility when a woman kills her batterer, it is *a fortiori* relevant to her credibility when she participates in robberies at her batterer's insistence."[34]

This was the first time the court indicated a willingness to accept the victimization defense strategy in a case in which the defendant and victim are strangers. And, as in the acquaintance case discussed earlier, the abuser in this case—the cause of Debra's victimization—is not the victim. Instead, Debra's victimization is used to explain and justify her actions toward innocent bystanders who are strangers to her.

In addition, in this case the court recognizes that the strategy should be accepted to support a duress defense because "the defense of duress is the same as self-defense—in both, the key issue is whether the defendant reasonably and honestly believed she was in imminent danger of great bodily harm or death."[35] Thus the court also expands on the types of defenses the strategy can be used to support.

Not only have the types of defendants using the strategy expanded, but the strategy is now accepted in cases in which the relationship between the defendant and the victim is more distant. Though initially applied to cases in which the defendant and victim are intimates, it has gradually expanded to cases in which they are acquaintances or even strangers. This expansion includes a recognition that the strategy can also be used when the victim of the crime is an innocent third party who is not the cause of the defendant's victimization.

"Victimless" Cases

The expansion has not stopped with the Romero "stranger case." The strategy has also been accepted in victimless crime cases—for example, incidents involving welfare fraud and drug distribution.[36] Arguably, these kinds of crimes have no victims, and therefore no relationship to consider between the defendant and the victim; or perhaps they involve a more abstract victim such as "the people" or "the state."

The drug distribution case of the *United States v Marenghi* exemplifies this further expansion.[37] The defendant was charged with conspiracy to possess and distribute a controlled substance. She offered a duress, or compulsion, defense based on the victimization defense strategy, arguing that she was physically abused by her boyfriend and coerced into participating in the offense. Again, the element of the strategy under contention was the proffered expert testimony on battered woman syndrome.

Although the appellate court did not rule directly that such testimony was admissible, it strongly indicated its willingness to admit such testimony, stating, "This Court cannot envision that such evidence [of battered woman syndrome] should be excluded in a duress defense."[38] Essentially, this indicated the court's willingness to accept the victimization defense strategy in support of a duress defense in a "victimless crime" case. Thus, not only has the victimization defense strategy been accepted in cases in which the defendant and victim are strangers; it has been recognized as a valid approach even when no victim exists.

These cases illustrate a second continuum along which the application of the strategy has extended. It can now be used in a variety of situations that are different from the original battered woman's self-defense context: situations involving more distant victim-offender relationships; situations in which the victim is not the cause of the defendant's victimization; and situations founded on claims of duress rather than self-defense. Notably, the judges in these cases legitimate their extensions of the strategy by explaining the similarities between these cases and battered woman's self-defense.

Expansion of Victimization

All of the cases discussed thus far share one feature—the type of social victimization to which the defendant is subjected. In all of them, the source of the social victimization is battering or physical abuse by a distinct individual (a boyfriend, husband, or parent), the type of social victimization highlighted by the first battered women's cases using the strategy.

However, several defendants have attempted to use a different type of social victimization as the basis for the strategy. In these cases, a specific abuser or specific injury is difficult to find. Instead, the social victimization is more abstract or generalized and the injury more psychological than physical—for instance, war trauma or social deprivation. Such forms of victimization are still "social" to the extent that their cause lies in the social environment. However, the specific individuals responsible for the victimization and the specific injuries suffered are more difficult to identify. These cases primarily proffer a victimization defense strategy based on expert psychological testimony about Post-Traumatic Stress Disorder (PTSD). Defendants recount histories of trauma and deprivation that lead them to suffer from PTSD, which in turn causes them to behave in unacceptable ways.

While the courts have not completely dismissed this form of the victimization defense strategy, the vast majority of cases relying on these abstract forms of social victimization have been rejected. Whereas cases forwarding the strategy based on physical abuse are increasingly being accepted by appellate courts, cases relying on deprivation or trauma have received a more tempered reception. Courts, then, seem to allow more types of defendants in more types of situations to claim victimization as an excuse, but they seem reluctant to expand on the definition of victimization itself. Victims are the abused of society, not the traumatized or deprived.

PTSD and the Victimization Defense Strategy

The term "Post-Traumatic Stress Disorder" (PTSD) was first used as an official diagnostic category in the third edition of the *Diagnostic and Statistical Manual of Mental Disorders* (*DSM-III*) published in 1980 (Erlinder 1983, 1984). As defined in the *DSM-III-R* (the revised third edition of the manual published in 1987), post-traumatic stress disorder develops "following a psychologically distressing event that is outside the range of usual human experience (i.e., outside the range of such common experiences as simple bereavement, chronic illness, business losses, and marital conflict)" (*DSM-III-R* 1987:247). Such "distressing events" include both natural disasters and traumas of human design, such as torture, war, and severe physical abuse.

The primary feature of PTSD is its delayed onset. Symptoms begin only after the original stressor has been terminated. Often symptoms do not appear until months, even years, after the end of the traumatic event. Symptoms of PTSD include the reexperiencing of the traumatic event, increased arousal (also called hypervigilance), and a numbing of general responsiveness (*DSM-III-R* 1987).

Post-traumatic stress disorder is different from most other psychological disorders in that the condition is "brought about by factors external to the person who experiences symptoms" (Erlinder 1983:30; see also Slovenko 1984). One legal analyst even commented that the development of PTSD by an individual should be recognized as a "social and political phenomenon, not just an intrapsychic one," and that those suffering from PTSD are "victims of powerful social and historical forces far beyond their control" (Schulz 1982:2404, 2402). Unlike most psychological disorders, then, a diagnosis of PTSD requires an understanding of the social causes of the disorder.

The history of the development of this particular diagnostic category is rooted in the stress produced in combat situations. Not recognized by the medical community until World War I, the symptoms now known as PTSD were then known popularly as "shell shock" (see Brotherton 1981 and Erlinder 1984 for a history of the term). Although similar diagnostic categories, such as "gross stress reaction" and "transient situational personality disorder," did appear in earlier versions of the *DSM*, the 1980 manual was the first to group all of the symptoms together under a single category (Erlinder 1983). Consolidation of the various categories into one in the 1980 *DSM* provided a single clear description of the disorder, making it easier to use in diagnosis, treatment, and legal proceedings (Erlinder 1984). Its inclusion in the *DSM-III* signaled its acceptance by the psychiatric community, providing legitimacy for its use in the courtroom (Burke 1980). Those defendants who were first to use expert psychological testimony on PTSD in court within the context of a criminal defense were almost exclusively Vietnam veterans (Scrignar 1988).

Soon after PTSD appeared in the *DSM-III*, criminal defendants began using it in court, primarily to support an insanity or diminished capacity plea (Brotherton 1981; Erlinder 1983). The typical situation in which evidence of PTSD was used were cases in which a Vietnam veteran committed a crime (for example, murder, burglary, fraud, or conspiracy) and later claimed that the action occurred while he was reexperiencing a combat situation. The veteran argued that he did not understand that what he was doing was criminal; he was merely reacting to a typical combat scenario. Evidence of PTSD would be proffered to explain how and why such "flashbacks" occur and the impact they have on the veteran.

A defense strategy based on PTSD incorporates all of the elements of the victimization defense strategy. According to legal scholars interested in this approach, a defense strategy based on PTSD should emphasize a number of key elements. First, the defense must establish that the defendant suffers from PTSD and that symptoms of the disorder were apparent, although undiagnosed, before the crime occurred (Scrignar 1988; Wellborn 1982). This is established through expert testimony by psychologists or psychiatrists who detail the symptoms experienced by the defendant. Second, the defense must provide an elaborate accounting of the traumatic events he experienced during war—injuries suffered, horrific actions witnessed and perpetrated (Erlinder 1984; Scrignar 1988).

These experiences are characterized rather abstractly as "war trauma."

Third, the defense offers an explanation of the psychological impact of such experiences on the mental state of the defendant, again in the form of expert testimony on PTSD (Scrignar 1988). Finally, the defense presents testimony about the defendant's mental state at the time of the crime, emphasizing any similarities between the crime scene and combat situations that could invoke a combat response from the defendant. This testimony serves to connect the underlying cause of the PTSD (social victimization in the form of war trauma) to the criminal act itself (Erlinder 1984; Scrignar 1988). With a victimization defense strategy based on PTSD, "it is possible to point to specific events to establish a causal link to client behavior. As a result, once PTSD is found to be a factor in client behavior, an attorney may present in a systematic and logical manner the events that brought about the acts in question" (Erlinder 1984:312–313).

Each of the elements of the victimization defense strategy is evident in this outline of the approach based on PTSD—the focus on the behavior of others in one's past, the recounting of past traumas (social victimization) suffered by the defendant, the presentation of expert psychological testimony on the impact of such trauma on the defendant, and the construction of the defendant as a victim not only of injuries and trauma but of an unjust war.[39]

The defense strategy based on PTSD is, therefore, functionally the same as the victimization defense strategy developed in battered women's self-defense cases. In fact, Erlinder (1983:43) noted the extent to which those using the PTSD defense strategy were indebted to the defense strategy used in battered women's cases: "The use of PTSD in this context . . . parallel[s] that of the 'battered spouse syndrome' that has been used to explain a female defendant's violent acts. . . . the existence of PTSD . . . make[s] the whole of a defendant's life relevant to show his state of mind at the time of the occurrence." However, the use of the strategy in this type of case is different in that the source of the social victimization is not physical battering by a specific individual. Instead, the cause of the victimization is more generalized and abstract—war trauma, shell shock, combat fatigue.

Acceptance or Rejection?

The use of the victimization defense strategy founded on PTSD has not been as successful as its use when based on physical abuse. While all of the original and expansion cases discussed thus far have involved social victimization in the form of battering, the acceptance of the argument in the form of PTSD has been much more limited.[40] Since 1980, appellate courts have reviewed numerous cases in which the defense has relied on the approach based on war-induced PTSD, usually in support of the defenses of insanity and self-defense. The overwhelming majority have been unsuccessful: appellate courts have affirmed the convictions,[41] indicating an unwillingness to recognize this form of the approach.

The only case in which courts provided some support for war-induced social victimization was in a case relying on a diminished capacity defense. In *Glass v Vaughn*,[42] the defendant was convicted of first-degree murder in the stabbing death of a woman with whom he had had a sexual relationship. On appeal, the defendant contended that his trial counsel was ineffective for not investigating a diminished capacity defense based on PTSD. The defendant testified to the traumatic events he experienced in Vietnam, and several witnesses attested to his "bizarre" behavior after his return. In addition, the court heard testimony from four mental health experts who all agreed that the defendant "suffered from PTSD at the time of the victim's death" as a result of his Vietnam experiences.[43]

The appellate court agreed with the defendant, concluding that the trial counsel was ineffective for not investigating a victimization defense strategy based on war-induced PTSD. The court ordered a new trial.[44] Although the use of the strategy in this case was accepted, it has not been supported in the majority of cases relying on war-induced PTSD, indicating that the expansion of the strategy in this context—a context in which the cause of the social victimization suffered by the defendant is more general and abstract (and physical injury less apparent)—is tenuous at best.

Aside from cases involving war-induced PTSD, the courts have considered a few cases involving PTSD caused by other types of generalized trauma. For example, in *State v Morgan*, the defendant, Felicia Morgan, attempted to admit testimony that she suffered from PTSD caused by years of growing up in an inner-city ghetto in which violence, deprivation, and fear were commonplace (to support a plea to a lesser charge of reckless homicide).[45] She claimed to have committed the homicide and robberies for which she was convicted while in the throes of a post-traumatic stress reaction. The appellate court refused to admit the testimony about PTSD as well as testimony about her general psychosocial history, thereby rejecting the use of the victimization defense strategy in this case.

The only appellate support for the use of the strategy based on generalized trauma of this type is found in *State v Fields*.[46] Here the court did indicate some acceptance of the strategy in support of an automatism defense. The automatism defense is also known as the defense of unconsciousness. The rationale behind this defense is that someone who "engages in what would otherwise be criminal conduct is not guilty of a crime if he does so in a state of unconsciousness or semi-consciousness" (LaFave and Scott 1986:382). An individual who is unconscious or semiconscious at the time that he commits a crime has not engaged in a voluntary act, an element necessary for criminal responsibility (LaFave and Scott 1986).

In the Fields case, the defendant was convicted of the first-degree murder of an acquaintance. During the trial, the defendant and others testified that he had endured a traumatic childhood that included physical abuse. However, the part of his past that apparently traumatized him most significantly was an incident in which he was forced to shoot his stepfather to defend his mother from abuse.[47] The defense contended that as a result of this the defendant was mentally scarred. At trial, the defense argued that the situation in which Fields had murdered his friend was similar in many ways to this childhood event involving his stepfather, causing the defendant to dissociate.[48] In other words, the defendant was unconscious at the time that he murdered his friend. The defense offered expert psychological testimony that the defendant suffered from PTSD as a result of this traumatic childhood event to support this argument.

While the trial court refused to instruct the jury on the defense of automatism based on this testimony, the appellate court reversed this decision and ordered a new trial in which instructions on the unconsciousness defense were required. The court indicated that it based this decision on the expert's testimony about PTSD and the testimony of the family members about the defendant's childhood and history.[49]

Though the focus of the testimony in the Fields case was on the mental trauma caused by the childhood shooting and neglect and not the trauma of physical abuse, this is not a "pure" example of a case using the victimization defense strategy based on generalized social victimization. Physical abuse was a part of his victimization as well. Courts, then, still have not fully recognized the use of the strategy based on deprivation and mental/emotional trauma as the sole form of victimization. As such, the only appellate decision to accept the victimization defense strategy based on PTSD caused by generalized trauma remains *Glass v Vaughn*.[50] Courts do seem reluctant to expand the strategy to defendants suffering more abstract and generalized forms of trauma.

This reluctance becomes even more evident when one analyzes other cases that use the strategy involving PTSD. While the strategy has had limited acceptance in cases in which the PTSD is caused by war trauma or general social trauma, the strategy has been accepted in many cases in which the PTSD is caused by the physical abuse of an individual. Again, according to the *DSM-III-R* (1987), PTSD can be caused by a variety of traumatic events, including severe physical abuse. In fact, the *DSM-III-R* recognized battered woman syndrome as a subcategory of PTSD (Walker 1993). Several successful battered women's self-defense cases relying on the victimization defense strategy have offered expert psychological testimony on both battered woman syndrome and PTSD. These cases are functionally equivalent to the cases to which the victimization defense strategy was originally intended to apply, except for the addition of testimony about PTSD.[51]

Thus, courts are not hesitant to accept the strategy when founded on PTSD in general; only when the disorder is said to be caused by war trauma, deprivation, or social neglect, rather than physical battering. These cases, then, do represent an attempt to further expand the use of the victimization defense strategy; however, this dimension of expansion—to cases relying on types of social victimization other than physical abuse—is limited and tenuous.

The Lessons of Expansion

Evidently, more and more defendants have been able to use victimization as an excuse to responsibility over the past fifteen years—male defendants and children as well as females; defendants beaten by loved ones who strike back and defendants beaten by loved ones who choose innocent targets; defendants who act in self-defense, and while insane or under duress; defendants who victimize intimates, acquaintances, or complete strangers. The ranks of the "victims" who can use this approach have grown. Despite their increasing diversity, however, these defendants do share a common history. All of these victims were physically abused. Though defendants suffering from other forms of trauma have tried to avail themselves of this strategy, the courts seem clear: physical abuse is the only form of social victimization that will be accepted as a legitimate basis for the strategy. The law, then, is actually defining victimization and determining *who* is an acceptable victim. Yes, then, victims have joined the ranks of those excused from responsibility for their actions—but only certain victims.

Why? Why are victims of other forms of social victimization excluded from this process? I contend that the answer lies in our beliefs about the primacy of individual responsibility. The victimization defense strategy is successful in cases in which the social victimization is physical battering because these types of cases actually reconfirm the primacy of one-on-one harm and personal responsibility in the law. In such cases, the defendant can point to a single individual or number of distinct individuals who are responsible for her victimization. The battered woman, child, or man can identify the individual responsible for his or her abuse and subsequent actions. In turn, judges and juries can identify the specific individuals responsible for the physical abuse of the defendant and can shift the blame for the actions of the defendant to this other party. Though the recent extension of the strategy signals the inclusion of victims among those not responsible for misconduct, paradoxically, the expansion is limited to those cases that actually reconfirm the importance of individual responsibility in the law, albeit one step removed.

The lack of acceptance of the strategy in cases in which the type of social victimization is more abstract only supports this point. In these cases, the defendant cannot point to a specific individual who is the cause of his victimization. In essence, no single individual can be held responsible. Instead, the cause of the victimization is said to be a collective, such as war, society, or a bad neighborhood. These cases do not affirm the premise of individual responsibility, and are therefore rejected.

In other words, defendants who have been physically abused are allowed to reconstruct their identity and take on the victim status because they can identify their victimizers. In the PTSD cases, the defendants are not allowed to take on the victim identity because no specific victimizer exists. Instead, the defendant claims to be a victim of society, something that anyone could claim if allowed. A recognition of this type of social victimization is outside the legal framework of personal responsibility; if allowed, it could result in legal chaos.

Legally, then, the physically abused are victims who can use their status to alleviate responsibility for their harmful actions, while defendants suffering harm imposed by the collective cannot avail themselves of the same excuse. As such, we see the cultural understandings of responsibility changing as victims are added to the ranks of those we will excuse while reaffirming the primacy of individual responsibility in our legal system. The acceptance and expansion of the victimization defense strategy does not, then, mark the end of personal responsibility, as some critics have forewarned (Birnbaum 1991; Dershowitz 1994b). Rather, the process signals a redefinition of responsibility, a shift in whom we hold responsible and under what conditions, while at the same time maintaining individual responsibility as the cornerstone of the law. The concept of responsibility is both expanded and confirmed.

6

Moments of

Redefinition

in Law and

Culture

I began this book by asking a number of fundamental, and previously unasked, questions about a legal strategy—the abuse excuse—that was the subject of heightened media and public attention during the mid-1990s. In answering my own questions, I learned about the law and a new argument that is being offered in the courtroom, but I also learned something about culture in general. Those original questions served as a framework around which unfolded a story about responsibility, victimization, and the law.

What is the "abuse excuse"? More precisely called the victimization defense strategy, it is a relatively new defense argument that can be used to support self-defense, insanity, and duress pleas by focusing on a defendant's past social victimization as a way of explaining present behavior. The strategy is typically composed of four elements, including: testimony about the defendant's past relationships, a focus on the defendant's past suffering, expert testimony about the impact of that suffering on present actions, and attempts to reconstruct the identity of the defendant as that of "victim." As a result, this defense argument makes a defendant's entire life relevant to the question of her responsibility for the actions under investigation.

When was the strategy first used? When did it first develop? First developed as a formalized legal approach in the 1970s, defense attorneys tried to use it in three different types of cases—rotten social background cases, brainwashing cases, and battered women's self-defense cases. Only in the last of these was the strategy accepted. Because of the concentrated efforts of a group of legal reformers who drew on organizational resources and successfully tied the strategy to broader cultural concerns over gender inequality and female victimization, the strategy was recognized as a viable new approach in battered women's self-defense cases. Today, this is one of the first defense approaches considered in cases of battered women who kill their abusers.

How is it used now? While still used in these battered women's cases, the strategy has also been accepted for use by battered men and children, as well as by battered individuals who kill innocent acquaintances or strangers instead of their abusers. This is now an argument available to individuals who have been physically abused who find themselves in a wide variety of situations relying on a variety of defenses. Despite this increasing diversity, the fundamental argument has remained the same: past abuse and victimization shape a defendant's present perceptions and behavior. As a result, the defendant should be relieved of responsibility for those actions.

What is it about this strategy that gets people upset? This approach appears to attack the cornerstones of the American legal system—free will and individual responsibility. In effect, a defense argument based on this strategy tries to persuade a judge and jury that the defendant is not responsible for his actions because those actions are not a result of free will. The behavior is, in fact, determined by outside social forces beyond the defendant's control. Given that legal and cultural understandings of responsibility assume free will, allowing us to blame and punish individuals for their misconduct, this strategy shakes these fundamental beliefs, causing anger and resistance. If behavior is determined by outside forces, anyone can argue that he is not responsible. If no one is held responsible, what is to prevent crime from burgeoning into an epidemic?

This, of course, is the same anger and resistance elicited any time a defense argument is founded on determinism. Take for example the continued controversy over the legitimacy of the insanity defense. While on the surface such fears and concerns may seem justified in relation to this new strategy, a more in-depth look at the success and expansion of the strategy reveals that, in fact, it does not represent the triumph of social determinism, nor the abandonment of individual responsibility. Though it requires a focus on past social victimization, the strategy also requires that the psychological impact of this past victimization be explained by an expert witness in psychology or psychiatry.[1] The effect of these outside social forces, then, must be filtered through the psychological model long accepted in the courtroom. The courts are willing to recognize social determinism if and only if it can be explained as impacting on the psychological functioning of the defendant. Without the psychological component, social determinism in itself is not an acceptable excuse from responsibility. In addition, the courts have made clear that defendants cannot claim just any form of social determinism—social victimization—and be excused. Courts have only recognized physical battering as the type of victimization worthy of consideration; they have not accepted arguments pointing to war trauma or social deprivation. Given these limitations, this strategy does not represent the wholesale recognition of social determinism in the law.

As a result, the success of the approach does not indicate the demise of individual responsibility. True, it does signal a redefinition of responsibility. Victims have been included in the ranks of those who can, in some circumstances, relieve themselves of responsibility for their actions. However, as already discussed, this inclusion is limited, and in a certain way. Only individuals suffering from a particular form of social victimization—physical abuse—can use this argument; other "victims" are held accountable. In addition, only those defendants who can identify their specific victimizers are legally defined as "victims." Defendants claiming to be the victims of war or society point to no specific individual that can be held accountable for their actions. Thus, though the attribution of individual responsibility is one step removed in these cases, the dimensions along which the use of the strategy has expanded actually confirm the primacy of individual responsibility. Responsibility is redefined but not abandoned.

What, then, does it mean for our society that a new defense based on victimization can now be used successfully in court? One could argue that this change in law is merely an isolated legal development that is in no way related to broader cultural changes. However, I disagree. Instead, I contend that the law can be used as a window into the larger culture: law can provide "a view of the way things are" (Geertz 1983:184). Legal definitions of responsibility are, in part, codifications of cultural definitions of responsibility. This does not mean that the law merely reflects the culture; the process is much more complicated than that. In this case, the feminist reformers drew heavily on cultural themes to develop the battered woman's self-defense strategy; therefore, through their diligence and the support they were given, these elites were able to institutionalize a new defense strategy that was directly tied to cultural themes of inequality, victimization, and a new definition of womanhood. However, the process does not end there. By recognizing and extending the strategy, the courts make explicit the connection between victimization and the alleviation of responsibility, which in turn contributes to the broader culture of victimization. Law and culture are intertwined in a mutually reinforcing exchange.

I see these two as inextricably linked. Changes in law, then, can be indicative of changes in culture. The increasing recognition of the victimization defense strategy as a viable defense argument for the physically abused marks a shift in cultural understandings of responsibility. Victims can excuse themselves from responsibility, but again only certain victims. The redefinition process is limited.

In many ways, the law is telling a story of a culture struggling with a new identity—the identity of "victim." Who are "victims" anyway? Gradually, those in and out of the courtroom have come to recognize that the answer to this question is not as straightforward as once believed. Victims, after all, are social constructions. Individuals are not objectively "victims"; they are labeled as such by others. "Victims" are produced through a descriptive and interactional process in which some people and groups come to be assigned the victim status while others do not (Holstein and Miller 1990).

Victims are produced daily in the media, in the medical and mental health communities, and in the criminal justice system. And victims are created in the courtroom as well. To a great extent, courts are concerned with determining who suffered injury (who is the victim), what is the extent of the injury inflicted (what is the degree of victimization), and who is responsible for imposing the injury (who is the victimizer). Once these issues are decided and the victim label applied, the court determines to what extent the victimizer is accountable for the injury and assigns punishment in kind.

However, the definition process taking place in the courtroom need not always work in this way. Courtroom processes need not always produce a single victim who suffered injury at the hands of the offender who is on trial. Because "victim," and "offender" for that matter, are socially constituted identities, these labels can be applied to anyone in the courtroom. The use of the victimization defense strategy is a case in point. The purpose of the strategy is to alter the identity of the person on trial. While pretrial proceedings and the prosecution have labeled the defendant as "offender," the defense seeks to reconstitute the identity of the defendant as that of "victim" by using the victimization defense strategy. For example, cases using the battered woman's self-defense strategy were the first routinely to win acceptance of the reconstruction of the responsible victimizer as the justified victim. Thus the courtroom becomes an arena for this struggle over definition and the application of the victim status.

One consequence of this definitional struggle is the establishment of a dichotomy (some would say a false dichotomy) between "victim" and "victimizer," as if these two terms are mutually exclusive. Few, if any, consider that one could be both a victim and a victimizer, both a victim and an offender.[2] Instead, someone is either an offender and therefore guilty, or a victim and therefore innocent. A "guilty victim" seems to have become a categorical impossibility.

This, of course, becomes one of the most significant reasons to take on the victim identity. Whereas victimization was considered to be a stigma of sorts in the past, connoting helplessness and passivity, now the victim identity confers innocence. Victims are innocent; they are people who have suffered some injury or injustice not of their own making. If they are innocent, they cannot also be guilty. If their misdeeds are born out of their innocence and victimization, they cannot be held responsible.

The institutionalization and expansion of the victimization defense strategy signals this process.[3] More and more, defendants attempt to reconstruct themselves and their histories to claim the victim identity *because* this identity has proven to be useful in explaining their behavior and alleviating their responsibility. As victims of past abuse and suffering, they are innocent of the condition that produced their misdeeds, and so should not be held responsible for those misdeeds.

This redefinition goes on outside the courtroom as well. The addiction industry continues to grow as forms of deviance are relabeled as diseases (for example, drug-taking, overeating, gambling), which in turn redefines deviants as victims (Peele 1989; Rieff 1991). Changes in personal injury and product liability law further increase the ranks of victims who can (though not always) downplay their own negligence to receive compensation for their victimization (Olson 1991; Sykes 1992a). And the expansion in "rights" claims continually adds to the victim category those who have been discriminated against or mistreated (Etzioni 1993; Glendon 1991). Interestingly, while many condemn the use of the victimization defense strategy in the courtroom, many others pursue similar strategies in other areas outside the courtroom. Thus, the struggles taking place within the law are struggles being fought throughout society—struggles over identity and responsibility.

The institutionalization of the victimization defense strategy is telling another story as well—a story about the redefinition of womanhood in late twentieth-century America. The initial success of the approach in battered women's cases not only represents a significant victory for the feminist reformers who developed the approach, but also a victory for the model of womanhood they consciously incorporated into the strategy. The "woman as person"—equal, rational, and victimized on occasion—finds a place in the law with the acceptance of this approach. She is of course also finding a place in the economy, family, political structure, and education system at about the same time. During this period, culture was getting acquainted with the "woman as person."

As such, the law and culture were getting acquainted with a new point of view as well. As Schneider and Jordan (1981:4) point out about the development of the battered woman's self-defense strategy, the purpose of the strategy was to incorporate "women's experiences and perspectives into existing concepts of criminal law." The intention was to provide a legally viable forum in which women could tell their stories and explain their actions from their own points of view, actions that they believed to be reasonable and justified given their histories and perspectives. To accommodate this new perspective, courts had to move away from what were considered the "objective" standards of self-defense: the reasonable man standard, the proportionality requirement, and the imminence requirement. The courts replaced these objective standards with more subjective criteria that examine each defendant's behavior from his or her own point of view. Under these conditions, the reasonableness of the woman's actions, the proportionality of her response, and her belief about the imminence of the threat are all judged from her perspective, given her unique physical characteristics and social experiences. Equality under the law, then, requires that courts realize that women and men may, in fact, act differently in similar situations.

While this change in the law is significant for the recognition of the woman's point of view, it also opens the door to the further acknowledgment of other perspectives. In other words, the jury must consider the woman's perspective when judging her actions. But the jury must also take into account the child's perspective when judging his actions, or the inner-city youth's perspective when judging hers. As a result, the subjectification of the law paves the way for the expansion of the strategy to more and more defendants seeking to explain their actions from their own points of view. Again, this legal shift serves as a microcosm of society, as our culture has become familiar with not only the woman's point-of-view, but that of the African American, the Hispanic, the poor, and the disabled. The attempt to embrace multiculturalism is nothing but an effort to recognize the diversity of perspectives that exist in the United States.

When using this legal change as a window, we see a great deal—several moments of redefinition. We see a culture struggling with new definitions of victimization, responsibility, and womanhood, and embracing a diversity of perspectives on life in America. How was all of this redefinition achieved? It all boils down to the initial efforts of those feminist advocates who worked in such a comprehensive way to develop a theoretically and practically accessible strategy. By garnering organizational support, they put in place a mechanism to ensure the widespread dissemination of their approach. By linking their strategy to the broader cultural issues discussed thus far, they created a legal approach that was recognizable by the layman. The battered woman's self-defense strategy was not a legal argument that existed in legal isolation: instead, the reformers relied on its connections to the cultural landscape for its acceptance and success.

No doubt this model can be replicated to promote the successful institutionalization of any strategy both inside and outside of the courtroom. Inside the legal arena, other legal scholars fighting for the acceptance of a unique legal argument could learn from the feminist advocates. One new approach well-situated to take advantage of this model is the "culture defense." This is a relatively new defense strategy typically offered by immigrants who have broken an American law. "The theory underlying the defense is that the defendant, usually a recent immigrant to the United States, acted according to the dictates of his or her 'culture,' and therefore deserves leniency" (Volpp 1994:57). The defense often offers expert testimony by an anthropologist to explain the cultural context guiding the defendant's actions. Only offered in a few trial cases and even fewer appellate courts, this approach has yet to be organized into a "singular, formalized defense" (Volpp 1994:57; see also Anon. 1986; Kotake 1993).

Given the increase in immigrant populations of late and the growing emphasis on multiculturalism in our society, this strategy could easily be linked to broader cultural concerns about the need to recognize and respect a diversity of cultural heritages. A group of legal scholars interested in issues of diversity could work on behalf of immigrant populations to formalize this approach by replicating the many efforts of the feminist reformers. Theoretically, the strategy could be tied to cultural themes of inequality and the need to respect diversity, while practically reformers could garner organizational support to back a host of activities, such as developing a consistent and singular strategy, writing about the approach, teaching it to students, soliciting opinions from other legal scholars, developing specific legal materials, and disseminating information. Again, the goal would be to make the strategy both theoretically and practically accessible. Though judges and jurors would be resistant at first, as they already have been to some extent, engaging in these activities would certainly increase the probability of acceptance in the long term.

This model would also be useful in fighting for the institutionalization of particular strategies in other arenas. For example, mental health professionals could engage in these activities to advocate for the inclusion of new mental disorders in the *Diagnostic and Statistical Manual of Mental Disorders*. Or justice professionals could rely on the model to lobby for and execute changes in policing practices. In fact this framework could be used to initiate any changes in policies, rules, laws, or practices. The type and breadth of activities in which these elites engaged to achieve their goal can be instructive to many who are attempting to produce similar change.

In the end, the development and expansion of the victimization defense strategy tells us many things about the society in which we live. We find ourselves at the nexus of a variety of changes as we struggle with new definitions of responsibility, of victimization, and of womanhood. We struggle with how to recognize new perspectives and points of view without abandoning individual responsibility altogether. And we learn how to effect legal and social change in accordance with our own definitions of the way law and culture should be.

Notes

1   *Responsibility and the Culture of Victimization*

1. The brothers actually claimed "imperfect self-defense." This defense is based on the honest but *unreasonable* belief that the use of force is justified to defend one's life (Dressler 1987:199). A successful defense of imperfect self-defense results in a conviction for manslaughter rather than murder. Thus, the defense succeeds only in mitigating responsibility, rather than fully justifying the accused's actions.
2. See the following: Arenella 1993; Birnbaum 1991; Dershowitz 1994b; Fletcher 1994; Goldberg 1994; Gregory 1994; Hughes 1993; Jacobs 1994; Kakutani 1994; Leo 1988, 1990, 1992a, 1992b, 1994; Lewis 1994; Mauro 1994; Morrow 1991; Rieff 1991; Robinson 1994; Slade 1994; Staples 1994; Sykes 1992a, 1992b; Taylor 1991, 1994.
3. The victimization ethos has also received substantial coverage on television news broadcasts, such as: CNN's *Sonya Live, CNN & Company,* and *Crossfire;* ABC's *Nightline* and *20/20;* and NBC's *Dateline.* However, as is the case with the talk shows, these broadcasts usually focus on sensationalized court cases and include little systematic analysis.
4. Aside from the popular press, the victimization theme has received attention in other forms of media as well. For example, the culture of victimization is the focus of a song on the Eagles' 1994 album, *Hell Freezes Over.* In "Get Over It," the band criticizes the media for drawing attention to individuals who attempt to shift blame by claiming the victim status.
5. Actually, victimization can be both a justifying and an excusing condition. Depending upon the type of legal defense being used, victimization can serve as either a justification or an excuse for the alleviation of responsibility. The legal differences between these two conditions will be addressed in detail in chapter 2. To avoid confusion and awkwardness, victimization will generally be referred to as an excusing condition.
6. The insanity defense and victimization defense strategy are different in that the insanity defense is a separate defense, in and of itself, while the victimization defense strategy is a method of argument used within existing defenses, such as insanity or self-defense. However, both establish that certain categories of people—the mentally ill and

victims—should be excused from responsibility for their misconduct given certain circumstances.

7. In fact, only 1 percent of all felony indictments result in an insanity plea. Of that 1 percent that plead "Not Guilty by Reason of Insanity," only 23 percent result in acquittals. Thus, the insanity defense is rarely used and rarely successful (Steadman et al. 1993). Yet its recognition by the legal system is significant nonetheless. The existence of insanity as a legally recognized defense establishes that mental illness can be a legitimate excuse from responsibility.

8. To avoid awkward constructions, male and female pronouns will be used alternately throughout the book.

9. The following analyses have also used the law as an empirical indicator of broader social changes, following in the Durkheimian tradition: Friedman 1985; Glendon 1987, 1989; O'Donnell and Jones 1982; Okun 1986; Weitzman 1981.

10. I use the word "defense" here loosely. Legally speaking, premenstrual syndrome, battered woman's syndrome, and the like are not criminal defenses. These are, instead, the physical and psychological conditions used to support legally recognized criminal defenses of, say, insanity or self-defense. For example, an abused woman who has killed her abusive spouse may offer testimony about battered woman's syndrome to explain her actions and bolster her plea of self-defense.

11. The "injury" produced by the social victimization includes physical injuries such as bruises and broken bones, as well as more abstract injuries such as psychological trauma. While the type of injury may vary, cases relying on social victimization share a common feature: the cause of the injury can be found in the social environment (as opposed to one's genetic structure or mental functioning).

12. Falk (1996) refers to these social-environmental factors that influence behavior as "social toxins." See also Garbarino (1995) for a detailed discussion of the theory of social toxicity.

13. The term "won" is used here because several legal analysts have noted that cases such as the Osby and Menendez cases would have been considered "open and shut" cases ten to twenty years ago. Therefore, the fact that the defense avoided conviction in these cases can be seen as a victory (Dershowitz 1994b; Goldberg 1994). While Osby's first trial resulted in a mistrial, his second trial ended in a conviction for murder. However, commentators note that the victimization defense strategy based on "urban survival syndrome" was not used as prominently in his second trial (Falk 1996).

14. Another example of a defense strategy can be found in the trials of Damian Williams and Henry Watson, who were charged with the beatings of eight people (including Reginald Denny) during the Rodney King riots. To support a diminished capacity defense, the defense combined sociological expert testimony about "group contagion theory" with racialized overtones to explain why the defendants could not have thought about or planned their actions. Williams and Watson were not convicted of the most serious charges against them (Alfieri 1995).

15. For the purposes of this analysis, a victim is someone who has been

the object of "harmful, unfair treatment" in the form of oppression, deprivation, or suffering (Holstein and Miller 1990). However, as indicated by the fourth component of the victimization defense strategy, individuals are not objectively "victims." "Victims" are produced and socially constructed. See Holstein and Miller (1990) for a further discussion of the social construction of victimization.

16. Only on occasion, as in high-profile cases like the Patty Hearst case discussed later, are trial court transcripts published for public viewing. To obtain the trial transcript of a particular case, usually the researcher must write to the jurisdiction in which the trial took place. (Virginia alone has 31 circuits and 122 circuit courts.) In addition, cases are filed by name alone. They are not indexed by subject or type of case, making it difficult to request all cases of a particular type, such as all domestic violence cases.

17. Conversation with Jeff Tatum, attorney, 22 September 1995.

18. The search of both the law reviews and the appellate cases was aided by the use of the Lexis on-line computer service that indexes all published state and federal cases and statutes, a large number of law review articles, and a variety of other legal materials.

2 Responsibility under the Law

1. The intent here is to provide an accessible overview of legal concepts and to familiarize the nonlawyer with important terms without overburdening him with confusing legal jargon. This discussion does not address the myriad philosophical debates over many of these terms nor the degree to which much of this varies by state and jurisdiction. For a more detailed analysis of the variety of meanings for legal terms and the host of exceptions to and variations in these rules, see Dressler's (1987) and LaFave and Scott's (1986) criminal law textbooks.

   The element of *mens rea* serves as a good example of the complexity of these legal terms. *Mens rea* can be interpreted in a number of ways, including "intentionally," "negligently," "restlessly," "willfully," "knowingly," and "with malice" (Dressler 1987:98–106). In addition, those states using the *Model Penal Code* (American Law Institute 1985) rely on a different set of meanings for the term. However, the reader need not fully understand these nuances of meaning to follow the arguments developed here.

2. This requirement also includes cases in which the defendant fails to act when she has a duty to do so.

3. Strict liability and vicarious liability offenses are excluded from this general requirement. Strict liability offenses allow for conviction and prosecution without proof of *mens rea*. Vicarious liability offenses are those in which someone can be punished for the actions of someone else—for example, when a corporate chief is held responsible for the crimes of an employee (see Dressler 1987:117).

4. The other two categories of true defenses are specialized defenses and extrinsic defenses. Specialized defenses apply only to a limited number of crimes, unlike justifications and excuses that can be used for all

crimes. For example, "legal impossibility" is a defense only to the crime of attempt: attempt occurs when someone has formed the intent to commit a crime and has taken substantial steps towards the completion of that crime. The "abandonment" defense only applies to the crimes of attempt and conspiracy (the agreement of two or more persons to commit an unlawful act). Extrinsic defenses result in the acquittal of the defendant based on factors unrelated to the actor's behavior or blameworthiness. "Statue of limitations" and "diplomatic immunity" are examples of extrinsic defenses (Dressler 1987).

5. The designation of conduct as justified or excused also has implications for determining the burden of proof and accomplice liability (Dressler 1987).

6. However, some legal scholars do not find sufficient cause to maintain the conceptual difference between these two terms. Drafters of the *Model Penal Code* do not recognize a difference between a justification and an excuse defense (Dressler 1987:188).

7. Apparently, some scholars do debate whether necessity is a justification or an excuse defense (Moore 1985; Robinson 1982). The defense of necessity is also known as the "lesser-evils defense." An actor may use a necessity defense if he violates the law to avoid a more serious harm created by natural forces. For example, an actor who burns another's property to create a fire line to stop a wildfire from spreading can avail himself of the necessity defense.

8. In some cases, insanity is offered as a case-in-chief defense to negate the *mens rea* element of the crime (Dressler 1987:313–314).

9. This discussion of legal defenses relies heavily on two legal textbooks: Joshua Dressler's (1987) *Understanding Criminal Law* and the second edition of LaFave and Scott's (1986) *Criminal Law*. These texts are widely accepted in the field. LaFave and Scott's text is frequently cited in other texts (including Dressler's), and Dressler is a noted and well-published legal scholar. Unless otherwise noted, the legal commentary on these three defenses comes directly from these two sources.

10. This defense is available in a minority of jurisdictions (Dressler 1987).

11. The first trial of both brothers ended in hung juries with half of the jurors voting for first-degree murder and half for manslaughter. Lyle and Eric Menendez were convicted of first-degree murder at their second trial and sentenced to life in prison.

12. Because of its use in a few high-profile cases involving bizarre crimes or high-status victims, the public is left with the impression that the insanity defense is frequently used and used primarily in homicide cases. Neither impression is correct. Only 1 percent of felony indictments claim an insanity plea (much less win one—see Steadman et al. 1993), and 86 percent of insanity pleas are offered in cases involving nonviolent offenses (cited in Dressler 1987:289).

13. As happens in most cases in which a defendant is acquitted by reason of insanity, Lorena Bobbitt was immediately committed to a state hospital for psychiatric observation. After approximately one month, the court ordered her conditional release from that facility (Fletcher 1995).

14. Aside from the M'Naghten rule and the MPC test, the insanity defense

has been instituted in a number of other forms as well. The "product test" or Durham rule was established in a landmark case in 1954 (*Durham v United States*, 214 F.2d 862 [1954]). The Durham rule states simply that an actor is excused if the crime is the product of a mental disease or defect. This test draws a direct causal connection between the mental disease and the act in question. The actor is excused only if the mental disease directly produces the criminal conduct; if the actor was not diseased, the act would not have been committed.

This decision sparked controversy because it was a substantial departure from previous formulations of insanity. Among the controversies over this version of the defense, critics argued that *Durham* failed to define the key phrase "mental disease or defect," leaving this power over definition to mental health experts. As a result, the Durham rule gave too much power to psychiatrists, power that belonged in the hands of jurors. Essentially, the product test allowed for a psychiatrist to decide the guilt or innocence of a defendant, thereby usurping the power of the jury. A psychiatrist merely needs to testify that the defendant suffers from a condition, that the condition is a mental disease, and that the condition caused the defendant to commit the crime. This leaves nothing for the jury to do but decide whether they will accept or reject the expert's testimony. The Durham rule received little support from other courts and was overruled in 1972 (*United States v Brawner*, 471 F.2d 969, 973 [1972]).

A minority of states currently do provide another alternative for the insanity defense known as a plea of "guilty but mentally ill." In states that recognize this alternative, a jury has four verdicts available to choose from in an insanity case: guilty, not guilty, not guilty by reason of insanity, and guilty but mentally ill. A verdict of "guilty but mentally ill" means that the jury believes the defendant was guilty of the crime but mentally ill at the time of the incident. If such a verdict is returned, the defendant is given the sentence attached to a guilty verdict. However, the defendant is remanded to a psychiatric care facility rather than immediately confined in prison. If the defendant is cured before the sentence is completed, he spends the remainder of the sentence in prison. If the defendant is not cured during the sentence period, he is released.

Finally, a limited number of states provide a diminished capacity defense (also called the "diminished responsibility" or "partial responsibility" defense) as a true defense for the crime of murder only. Under this defense, evidence that the defendant suffers from an abnormal mental condition short of insanity can mitigate a murder charge to manslaughter.

This defense attempts to recognize that both moral responsibility and mental illness exist on a continuum. Criminal responsibility is not an "all or nothing" condition, and people may be sane but still mentally abnormal. Therefore, this legal concept attempts to match the degree of criminal responsibility to the degree of mental instability, providing a tempered alternative to the insanity defense.

15. *M'Naghten's Case*, 10 Cl. & F. 200, 8 Eng. Rep. 718 (1843).

16. *Model Penal Code*, Section 4.01 at 178–179.
17. 376 A.2d 827, 832 (1977).
18. See for example: *Ibn-Tamas v United States*, 407 A.2d 626, 635–639 (1979), *reversed and remanded*, 455 A.2d 893 (1983), *aff'd; State v Kelly*, 97 N.J. 178, 478 A.2d 364 (1984); and *Smith v State*, 247 Ga. 612, 277 S.E.2d 678 (1981).
19. See the following cases for discussion of experts' qualifications: *Ibn-Tamas v United States*, 407 A.2d 626 (1979), *rev'd on remand and aff'd*, 455 A.2d 893 (1983); *Commonwealth v Craig*, 783 S.W.2d 387 (1990).
20. Faigman and Wright (1997) argue that advocates for battered women never provided evidence that such myths and stereotypes actually existed. According to Faigman and Wright, research on battered woman syndrome is an excellent example of "bad" science. However, because of the work of political advocates and lax judicial standards, such testimony has been allowed in court.
21. 293 F. 1013, 1014 (1923).
22. 407 A.2d 626, 638 (1979).
23. Again, Faigman and Wright (1997) would contend that this difficulty in proving the reliability of the research was primarily because it was, in fact, unreliable research.
24. *Ibn-Tamas v United States*, 407 A.2d 626, 638 (1979).
25. See *Smith v State*, 247 Ga. 612, 277 S.E.2d 678, *on remand*, 159 Ga.App. 183, 283 S.E.2d 98 (1981).
26. 509 U.S. 579 (1993).

3   *Deprivation, Brainwashing, and Battering*

1. A few legal scholars have noted the similarities among these defenses; however, none have actually detailed what those similarities are (Delgado 1985; Vuoso 1987).
2. While the reliance on social victimization within the context of a criminal defense is new, defense attorneys commonly refer to a history of victimization during the sentencing stage. As Falk notes (1996:801), "courts' use of the types of information upon which these [defense] theories are premised at the time of sentencing is not unique or unusual."
3. The fact that the insanity defense is so rarely used and rarely successful lends further credence to the argument that the law is generally resistant to determinist defense theories. See chapter 1, note 7.
4. *M'Naghten's Case*, 8 Eng. Rep. 718 (1843). For a more detailed history of the insanity defense dating back to the seventh century, see Skeen 1983.
5. See the discussion about medical testimony and the insanity defense in *Washington v United States*, 390 F.2d 444 (1967).
6. For paranoia, see *State v Elsea*, 251 S.W.2d 650 (1952); for senility, see *State v Hadley*, 65 Utah 109, 234 P. 940 (1925); for epilepsy, see *Walsh v People*, 88 N.Y. 458 (1882) and *State v Wright*, 112 Iowa 436, 84 N.W. 541 (1900).

7. 471 F.2d 969, 995 (1972). While it recognized that one's background and environment affect one's behavior, the court in this decision was unwilling to adopt a "broad 'injustice' approach to criminal behavior." The court concluded that all determinist arguments about behavior must be filtered through the medical model provided by the insanity defense, thus explicitly rejecting the validity of social determinism while supporting biological and psychological determinism.
8. 407 A.2d 413, 416 (1979).
9. *State v Pagano*, 242 S.E.2d 825, 826 (1978); *State v Nuetzel*, 606 P.2d 920, 923 (1980).
10. This is the entire transcript of the original trial.
11. 471 F.2d 923, 959 (1973), Bazelon concurring in part and dissenting in part.
12. 390 F.2d 444 (1967).
13. *United States v Alexander and Murdock*, 471 F.2d 923 (1973).
14. *Id*. at 928–930; see also Delgado 1985:20–21.
15. *Id*. at 959, 960.
16. *Id*. at 958, 959.
17. *Id*. at 958–959. However, the expert also testified that this "abnormal mental condition" could not be labeled a mental illness, the type of defect upon which an insanity defense rests. The defense concurred, stating that the defendant " 'did not have a mental disease in the classic sense' " (at 959). Thus the defense was left to argue an insanity defense that did not fit into the medical model. In other words, the defense argued that Murdock's mental functioning was impaired because of his background and that impairment, though short of mental illness, should relieve him from responsibility for his actions. This, as discussed earlier, became an important premise of proponents of the RSB defense: insanity defenses should be expanded beyond the medical model and allowed to include all factors (not just biological factors) that produce mental impairment.
18. *Id*. at 960.
19. *Id*. at 959. Cited from the original trial transcript.
20. *Id*. at 959.
21. *Id*. at 960.
22. *Id*. at 960.
23. *Id*. at 960.
24. These six articles include: Bazelon 1976a, 1976b; Diamond 1973; Gross 1973; Morris 1968; Morse 1976.
25. Delgado 1985; Dressler 1989; Kadish 1987; Moore 1985; Pillsbury 1992; Vuoso 1987; Wright 1994.
26. Gabel and Harris (1982:404–405) do cite a *trial* court case that apparently used the RSB defense successfully—*United States v Schneider*, Cr. No. 74–241 SC (N.D. Cal. 1975). Schneider was accused of committing a number of bank robberies while on parole. His defense was predicated on the theory that his childhood in a tough, working-class neighborhood and his violent prison experiences caused him to develop a schizoid personality, which in turn produced his criminal behavior. The jury acquitted him by reason of insanity.

However, because this is a trial court case, the success of the defense here does *not* establish its legitimacy as a matter of law. Only appellate cases determine law.

27. Butler notes that black trial juries often acquit black defendants for much the same reason outlined by the RSB defense: a history of racial and social discrimination predisposes black juries to be suspect of the criminal justice system and to rebel against this historical inequity by exercising their power to "emancipate some guilty black outlaws" (1995:679). Butler goes on to advocate for this form of jury nullification in cases involving nonviolent minority offenders.

While this does provide some evidence for the popularity of "rotten social background" as an excuse or justification in some minority communities, Butler presents no evidence that this was the premise of the defense strategy in these cases. In fact, he seems to be saying that the jurors actually believed the defendants to be guilty but imposed their own brand of popular justice at the end of the trial. In such circumstances, the RSB defense is best understood as a jury strategy, rather than a defense strategy. Even as an occasionally successful jury strategy, it is unlikely that such an approach would be recognized by an appellate court and become a matter of law. Thus, while they speak to the resonance of the RSB arguments within certain communities, such cases of jury nullification do not directly relate to this analysis of defense strategies.

Butler could, however, make use of the framework developed here to push for support of his jury nullification strategy. With the help of some high-profile advocates with organizational support and a resource base, he could have some success in promoting this new jury strategy.

28. This defense resurfaced in 1994 after attorneys for Colin Ferguson, the black man who killed six people on the Long Island Railroad, announced that they planned to use "black rage" as Ferguson's defense. For a discussion of this case, see Mills 1994; Page 1994; and Sneirson 1995. Ferguson eventually declined to use this strategy, fired his lawyers, and represented himself. He was convicted and sentenced to six life sentences (Milton 1995).

29. 471 F.2d 923 (1973).

30. One could argue, in fact, that this is exactly what happened in April 1987 when Bernhard Goetz was tried for the 1984 shooting of four young black men on a New York subway. In a highly publicized trial, Goetz argued that he had reacted in self-defense after being approached by the youths and asked for five dollars. Having been previously mugged in 1981, Goetz explained his fear of enduring another such incident, which is also why he began carrying a gun. The defense he offered could be described as a "white rage" argument within the context of self-defense.

The prosecution countered that Goetz had not acted reasonably or justifiably in this case. Rather than responding to a perceived imminent threat from the youths (as Goetz argued), the prosecution argued that Goetz was a mentally unstable vigilante who reacted to the race and youth of his victims. This argument, however, was lost on the jury who convicted Goetz of one count of criminal possession of a weapon but acquitted him of the more serious charges of attempted murder (see Fletcher 1988 for a detailed discussion of this case).

While this case provides an example of trial-level support for the use of this strategy, I could find no support for the use of "white rage" arguments at the appellate level. Harris (1997) provides a more detailed look at the "white rage" defense, including a discussion of an additional successful use of the defense at the trial level.

31. As a separate defense, black rage is no more successful than the RSB defense. Only five law review articles have been written specifically about black rage as a criminal defense, which is even fewer than the number of reviews written about RSB (see Copp 1995; Delgado 1985; Falk 1996; Gabel and Harris 1982; and Sneirson 1995). One successful appellate case using this strategy has been adjudicated—*Freeman v People*, 4 Denio 9 (N.Y. Sup.Ct. 1847) [discussed in Falk 1996; Harris 1997; Sneirson 1995]. However, this case was heard in 1846, more than a century before the concept of "black rage" was introduced by Grier and Cobbs (1968), and before lawyers considered it as a systematic basis for a defense strategy.

A black defendant, William Freeman, had been found sane and guilty of the murders of four white men. On appeal, the court reversed the conviction and remanded it for retrial on grounds that the sanity hearing was improperly conducted. Freeman died before the retrial was concluded. However, after his death, a second appellate court ruled that Freeman was insane "as a result of brutalization by whites" (Sneirson 1995:2253; see also Harris 1997). Since this time, no appellate use of the strategy has been successful.

In his recent book *Black Rage Confronts the Law* (1997), Harris discusses the development and use of this defense over the past century and describes several successful uses of the strategy at the trial level. However, given that no cases have reached the appellate level, this occasional recognition of legitimacy in trial courts has yet to receive the formal institutional endorsement provided by appellate rulings.

32. 174 Cal.App.2d 119, 125, 344 P.2d 342 (1959). The term was used only in passing in this case. Brainwashing was not the primary focus of the defense.

33. Lunde and Wilson (1977) report that ten servicemen who served in Korea were convicted and court-martialed for collaboration. Brainwashing was not specifically mentioned in any of these cases; however, three men did rely on defenses that were to some extent founded on an argument that a history of torture and indoctrination at the hands of their captors forced them to collaborate. For example, in *United States v Olson* (7 U.S.C.M.A. 460, 22 C.M.R. 250, 253–254, 258–259 [1957]), Olson argued that his act of collaboration occurred under duress. Olson testified that he had been repeatedly brutalized, starved, and fed propaganda during his internment in a Korean prison camp. At one point, his captors told him to write a number of articles that included anti-American and pro-Communist statements. Olson testified that they told him to "write or else." He claimed that he was

under duress when he wrote the articles because he truly thought, based on past experience, that they would beat him if he refused. The court convicted him, court-martialed him, and sentenced him to two years in prison, stating that despite his past experiences with his captors, he was not under immediate threat of serious harm at the time he wrote the articles. Therefore, a duress defense was not applicable. For similar cases, see *United States v Dickenson*, 6 U.S.C.M.A. 438, 20 C.M.R. 154 (1955); and *United States v Batchelor*, C.M. 377832, 19 C.M.R. 452 (1954). Each of these cases resulted in a conviction and court-martial.

Without a doubt, many servicemen who experienced these persuasion techniques were simply not charged with collaboration because the military chose to take into account the effect of the torturous ordeal they had endured, providing some support for the validity of the brainwashing argument. Yet it is also significant that the few cases brought to trial that relied on a modified brainwashing strategy resulted in conviction. These cases established, as a matter of law, that such a defense strategy was inadequate in this situation.

34. The legal concept of a brainwashing defense did get some attention during the Manson trials earlier in the decade. The three women—Patricia Krenwinkel, Susan Atkins, and Leslie Van Houten—convicted of the Tate and La Bianca murders alongside Charles Manson argued for a diminished capacity instruction to be given. They claimed that they were "slaves" and "robots" who did as Manson requested after being subjected to years of degradation, violence, and indoctrination by him; therefore, they did not possess the mental capacity required for murder. Their request was denied. Although this is quite similar to the brainwashing concept, the terms "brainwashing" and "coercive persuasion" were never used. See *People v Manson et al.*, 61 Cal.App.3d 102, 132 Cal.Rptr. 265, 274, 328 (1976).

35. *United States v Hearst*, 424 F.Supp. 307, 309 (1976).

36. *United States v Hearst*, 563 F.2d 1331, 1338 (1977).

37. *Id.* at 1338.

38. *Id.* at 1340.

39. *United States v Hearst*, 424 F.Supp. 307 (1976); *United States v Hearst*, 563 F.2d 1331 (1977). Hearst was sentenced to seven years in prison; President Carter commuted her sentence in 1979, after she had served two years.

40. See *People v Hoover*, 187 Cal.App.3d 1074, 231 Cal.Rptr. 203 (1986); *United States v King et al.*, 840 F.2d 1276 (1988); *Green v Scully*, 850 F.2d 894 (1988); *United States v Thomas and Richards*, 11 F.3d 1392 (1993).

41. *Neelley v State*, 494 So.2d 669 (1985).

42. *United States v Fishman*, 743 F.Supp. 713 (1990).

43. *Frye v United States*, 293 F. 1013, 1014 (1923). See the discussion of expert testimony in chapter 2.

44. Brainwashing has become the subject of another type of case recently. A flurry of litigation hit the courts in the 1980s regarding the techniques used by new religious movements to convert new members.

At the time, several "cults" were accused of brainwashing their members (Richardson 1996). In several cases, families hired deprogrammers to rid cult members of the belief systems they had adopted while part of the cults, often resulting in litigation brought by the cults, their former members, and the members' families. The majority of these legal actions involved civil litigation (Richardson 1996; Vermeire 1981).

However, a few criminal actions were pursued in cases in which the cult members were kidnapped by the deprogrammers (*United States v Patrick*, 532 F.2d 142 [9th Cir. 1976]; *People v Patrick*, 541 P.2d 320 [Colo. App. 1975]—see Note [1981] for other cases). In these cases, the defense usually pursued a necessity defense, often called a "lesser of two evils" defense. The primary defense argument is that kidnapping and deprogramming are lesser evils than leaving individuals in a "brainwashed" state within a cult (Richardson 1996). The results of the use of this strategy have been mixed (Note 1981), though it has been successful in several cases.

While brainwashing is obviously involved in such cases, it is not the foundation of the defense strategy. Parents and deprogrammers do not argue that they themselves were brainwashed, which caused them to kidnap cult members. Thus, while these cases involve the same issues, they do not rely on the victimization defense strategy.

45. However, more recent studies have shown that battered women are not often legally insane. If they do suffer from a mental illness, the illness typically subsides when the stressor (the abuse) is removed (Walker 1989).

46. For an example of acquittal on self-defense grounds, see *People v Giacalone*, 242 Mich. 16, 217 N.W. 758 (1928).

47. But see Maguigan (1991), who argues that the vast majority of battered women who kill their abusers do so during a confrontation.

Although the term "husband" is used here to refer to the abuser, battered women's self-defense cases are not limited to those women who kill their abusive husbands. The self-defense strategy is also used to defend women who kill abusive boyfriends, "live-ins," and common-law husbands.

48. Maguigan (1991) contends that it is not the law itself that is biased, but the application of that law by trial judges who fail to apply self-defense standards equally in battered women's cases.

49. The Project not only provided legal assistance for these women but also developed legal and educational materials to help attorneys and led training sessions about the defense strategy (Bochnak 1981a). Bochnak's edited volume *Women's Self-Defense Cases* (1981a), the primary written document about the work of the Project, provides detailed material about the strategy, as well as sample legal memoranda, jury instructions, and case lists.

50. Advocates for the strategy were primarily interested in recognizing that the actions of women who killed their abusers could be *justified*, which is why they focused primarily on the use of the strategy in the context of self-defense. However, they did concede that the facts of a

particular case might not support a self-defense plea, in which case use of the strategy within an insanity defense should be considered (Schneider and Jordan 1981). See Faith McNulty's *The Burning Bed* (1980) for a detailed account of the successful use of the victimization defense strategy within an insanity defense. See also *State v Felton*, 329 N.W.2d 161 (1983).

The success then of the strategy in battered women's cases and its failure in the RSB and brainwashing cases cannot be explained by differences in the defenses in which the strategy is used. In the RSB case, insanity was the primary defense; in the brainwashing cases, both insanity and duress were used; in battered women's cases, both insanity and self-defense were used.

51. See also *State v Crigler*, 23 Wash.App. 716, 719, 598 P.2d 739, 741 (1979). In this case, the court ruled that the defendant, who was claiming self-defense, was denied due process because the jury was not allowed to consider "all the surrounding circumstances which had occurred during the several months preceding the slaying."

52. Although most discussions of the battered woman's self-defense strategy assert the centrality of expert testimony (Bochnak 1981b; D'Emilio 1985; Rosen 1986; Thompson 1986; Walker 1989), Schneider (1980) cautions attorneys not to use it automatically. She argues that such testimony is not always necessary and sometimes can confuse the issues.

53. According to Faigman and Wright (1997), battered women advocates never provided evidence that such myths and stereotypes were actually generally held by the population.

54. Some courts have also resisted admitting evidence of past abuse to support a woman's self-defense claim. For example, evidence of an abuser's reputation for violence was excluded or limited in *State v Jacoby*, 260 N.W.2d 828 (1977); *State v Trombino*, 352 So.2d 682 (1977); *State v Crigler*, 23 Wash.App. 716, 598 P.2d 739 (1979) (cited in Schneider 1980:637).

55. Schneider goes on to argue that these two themes must be balanced. She fears that the defense strategy, especially testimony about battered woman syndrome, is being used only to emphasize the helplessness and passivity of the women. She claims that an overemphasis on passivity and victimization only undermines the centrality of the woman's reasonable perception of harm and reinforces stereotypes of women as incapable and unstable. See also Coughlin 1994.

56. 236 Kan. 461, 467, 693 P.2d 475, 479 (1985), cited in Schneider (1986c:198)—emphasis added.

57. 102 Misc.2d 775, 780–781, 424 N.Y.S.2d 626, 630 (1980), aff'd, 83 A.D.2d 719, 442 N.Y.S.2d 645 (1981), cited in Schneider (1986c:199)—emphasis added.

58. 97 N.J. 178, 478 A.2d 364 (1984), cited in Schneider (1986c:212)—emphasis added.

59. See Bochnak (1981a:289–300) for a table of trial cases using the strategy.

60. 555 A.2d 772 (1989).

61. The following account of their relationship is found in *Commonwealth v Stonehouse*, 555 A.2d 772, 774–780 (1989).
62. *Id.* at 781.
63. *Id.* at 781.
64. 494 Pa. 467, 472–473, 431 A.2d 949, 952 (1981).
65. *Commonwealth v Stonehouse*, 555 A.2d 772, 781 (1989).
66. *Id.* at 782.
67. *Id.* at 785.
68. *Id.* at 782.
69. The following cases using the strategy were reversed and remanded on appeal: *State v Kelly*, 97 N.J. 178, 478 A.2d 364 (1984); *State v Allery*, 101 Wash.2d 591, 682 P.2d 312 (1984); *Ibn-Tamas v United States*, 407 A.2d 626 (1979), *reversed and remanded*, 455 A.2d 893 (1983), *aff'd*; *Hawthorne v State*, 408 So.2d 801 (1982); *Smith v State*, 247 Ga. 612, 277 S.E.2d 678 (1981), *on remand* 159 Ga.App. 183, 283 S.E.2d 98 (1981); *People v Minnis*, 118 Ill.App.3d 345, 455 N.E.2d 209 (1983); *State v Anaya*, 438 A.2d 892 (1981); *People v Torres*, 488 N.Y.S.2d 358 (1985); *State v Leidholm*, 334 N.W.2d 811 (1983); *State v Hodges*, 239 Kan. 63, 716 P.2d 563 (1986); *Rogers v State*, 616 So.2d 1098 (1993); *People v Wilson*, 194 Mich.App. 599, 487 N.W.2d 822 (1992); *Bechtel v State*, 840 P.2d 1 (1992); *Commonwealth v Stonehouse*, 555 A.2d 772 (1989); *Commonwealth v Miller*, 634 A.2d 614 (1993); *State v Wilkins*, 407 S.E.2d 670 (1991); *Terry v State*, 467 So.2d 761 (1985); *Borders v State*, 433 So.2d 1325 (1983); *State v Hill*, 287 S.C. 398, 339 S.E.2d 121 (1986); *People v Humphrey*, 921 P.2d 1 (Cal. 1996); *Commonwealth v Zenyuh*, 307 Pa.Super. 253, 453 A.2d 338 (1982) [case reversed and defendant discharged].
70. Not all self-defense cases that use testimony on battered woman syndrome employ the entire defense strategy, but most of them do. Because testimony on battered woman syndrome is a key component of the strategy, acceptance of this testimony does indicate a general acceptance of the reasoning underlying the strategy as a whole.
71. *Bechtel v State*, 840 P.2d 1, 7 (1992).
72. The Lexis search that provided a substantial number of these reviews included all articles listed under the search "Battered Woman and Self Defense."

4   Extralegal Factors and the Success of the Battered Woman's Self-Defense Strategy

1. The Center for Constitutional Rights is a nonprofit legal and educational center founded in 1966. It provides materials and legal services for cases involving such issues as racial injustice, women's rights, criminal justice, and labor. The center co-sponsored the formation of the Women's Self-Defense Law Project, in which Schneider also participated (Bochnak 1981a).
2. Conversation with Elizabeth Bochnak, founder of the Women's Self-Defense Law Project, 15 January 1996.
3. *State v Wanrow*, 88 Wash.2d 221, 559 P.2d 548 (1977).

4. 97 N.J. 178, 478 A.2d 364 (1984).
5. This discussion of the "accessibility" of the strategy is indebted to Michael Schudson's (1989) discussion of the "retrievability" of culture.
6. The National Jury Project (NJP) is a nationwide trial consulting firm founded in 1975. NJP was established to provide social science research and expert advice to attorneys in a variety of civil and criminal trials. Members of NJP help lawyers use social science findings and theories in jury selection and case preparation (Krauss and Bonora 1983). See note 1 in this chapter for a description of the work of the Center for Constitutional Rights.
7. Conversation with Elizabeth Bochnak, 15 January 1996.
8. Conversations with Elizabeth Bochnak, 15 and 22 January 1996.
9. Funding sources included: the Abelard Foundation; the Lucius and Eva Eastman Fund, Inc.; the General Mills Foundation; the Ms. Foundation for Women, Inc.; the Playboy Foundation; the Women's Fund; the Board of Global Ministries of the United Methodist Church; the Coalition for Human Needs of the Episcopal Church Center; the Council on Women and the Church of the United Presbyterian Church, U.S.A.; and the Women's Birthday Offering of the Presbyterian Church, U.S.A.
10. See Greenberg (1994) for a history of the work of the NAACP Legal Defense and Education Fund. Harris (1997) does note that his efforts to publicize the black rage defense were encouraged by the National Lawyers Guild, though he does not specify the extent of that encouragement. He does explain that this was a pre-existing organization, not an organization specifically designed to support the use of this strategy. While this support was no doubt important to Harris's work on black rage, one can only assume that the support was limited because of other organizational demands.
11. *State v Wanrow*, 88 Wash.2d 221, 559 P.2d 548, 559 (1977). Wanrow had been convicted of killing a child molester who broke into her house during the night and made suggestive movements toward a child sleeping there (Gillespie 1989).
12. *Id.* at 559.
13. Schneider (1986c) goes on to argue that this tendency to focus only on the theme of victimization is a further indication of the tenacity of sexual stereotypes in our society. When two important themes are presented—woman as victim and woman as reasonable actor—courts choose to focus on the theme that adheres to past stereotypes.
14. This is not intended as a detailed history of the development and activities of the women's movement. Others have provided such histories quite adequately (Buechler 1990; Freeman 1975; Hole and Levine 1971; Rothman 1978; Ryan 1992). Neither do I wish to oversimplify or romanticize the unity or influence of the movement. Certainly, not all women participated in or supported the movement. Support was often divided by other social characteristics such as class and race, and even within the movement, activists disagreed as to goals and methods.

Nevertheless, one can still make valid generalizations about the movement's activities and influences. As Hole and Levine (1971:1) comment, on the whole those involved in the women's movement shared beliefs in "a fundamental re-examination of the role of women in all spheres of life, and of the relationships of men and women in all social, political, economic and cultural institutions," as well as a definition of women as an oppressed group.

15. The Equal Rights Amendment reads as follows: "Equality of rights under the law shall not be denied or abridged by the United States or by any State on account of sex."

16. I would, however, consider the possibility of a "floodgate effect." While the number of individuals claiming to have been brainwashed or even abused is limited, the proportion of the population that has suffered deprivation or discrimination is much greater. Recognition of the strategy in this type of case could open the "floodgate" to such cases, swamping the legal system and seriously undermining its reliance on free will. This perception could contribute to a rejection of the RSB strategy. However, it cannot explain the differential success of the brainwashing and battered woman's self-defense approaches.

5 Expanding the Use of the Victimization Defense Strategy

1. The second trials of Osby and the Menendez brothers resulted in the convictions of all of the defendants for murder. However, these cases still reinforce my contention that although the strategy is not always successful, it provides a new, potentially successful way of arguing cases that most would consider "open and shut." In spite of the fact that many legal analysts considered these to be "open and shut" cases and a second jury found the defendants guilty, the use of the strategy in the first trials did result in hung juries. In fact, in each case the victimization defense strategy was limited during the second trial. Jurors in the second trials were not presented with the full defense used in the first trials.

2. See Schudson (1989) for an interesting discussion of the importance of "institutional retention" to the success of ideas within a given culture.

3. *Commonwealth v Stonehouse*, 555 A.2d 772 (1989). See chapter 3 for a detailed summary of this case.

4. 617 A.2d 725 (1992).

5. *Id.* at 726.

6. *Id.* at 730.

7. *Id.* at 730.

8. *Id.* at 731.

9. *Id.* at 732.

10. 682 P.2d 991 (1984).

11. *Id.* at 995–996.

12. *Id.* at 1008.

13. *Id.* at 996.

14. *People v Cruickshank*, 105 A.D.2d 325, 484 N.Y.S.2d 328 (1985); *Whipple v State*, 523 N.E.2d 1363 (1988), *habeas corpus denied*, *Whipple v State*, 957 F.2d 418, *cert. denied*, 113 S.Ct. 218 (1992); *State v Reid*,

747 P.2d 560 (1987); *State v Holden*, No. 49566, slip op. (Ohio Ct. App. Sept. 26, 1985) [case reported in Van Sambeek 1988].

15. The term "battered child syndrome" was first used in an article by C. Henry Kempe and his colleagues in the *Journal of the American Medical Association* (1962). Originally, the term referred only to the physical injuries suffered by a child as a result of a pattern of prolonged abuse. During the 1970s, expert testimony, usually by a physician, on battered child syndrome was admissible in a number of different types of cases. For example, testimony on battered child syndrome was admissible in prosecutions of child abuse to establish that a child suffered from battered child syndrome (*People v Jackson*, 18 Cal.App.3d 504, 95 Cal.Rptr. 919 [1971]; *People v Ewing*, 72 Cal.App.3d 714, 140 Cal.Rptr. 299 [1977]). Such testimony was also allowed in homicide prosecutions to establish that a child's death resulted from battered child syndrome (*People v Sexton*, 31 Ill.App.3d 593, 334 N.E.2d 107 [1975]; *State v Loss*, 295 Minn. 271, 204 N.W.2d 404 [1973]).

However, not until the acceptance of the concept of battered woman syndrome in the legal and psychological communities did battered child syndrome also begin to refer to the psychological effects of battering on children. As legal analysts argued that battered child syndrome testimony was legally equivalent to battered woman syndrome testimony, defense attorneys began to pattern their defense strategies in parricide cases after the strategy used in battered women's self-defense cases. See Goldman (1994); Goodwin (1996); Moreno (1989); Smith (1992); and Van Sambeek (1988) for discussions of the use of expert testimony on battered child syndrome by the defense in parricide cases.

16. 121 Wash.2d 220, 850 P.2d 495 (1993).
17. *Id.* at 499.
18. *Id.* at 496.
19. *Id.* at 498.
20. *Id.* at 503.
21. *Id.* at 502.
22. Texas and Louisiana have enacted statutes addressing the admissibility of testimony on battered child syndrome. A second case allowing such testimony can be found in Louisiana: *State v Gachot*, 609 So.2d 269 (La.Ct.App. 1992), *cert. denied*, 114 S.Ct. 478 (1993). See Goodwin (1996) for a discussion of recent trends.
23. Some critics argue that Eric and Lyle Menendez cannot be described as children. At the time of the murders, Eric was 18 and Lyle was 21 (Fletcher 1995).
24. For spouses and ex-spouses: *Ibn-Tamas v United States*, 407 A.2d 626 (1979); *State v Kelly*, 97 N.J. 178, 478 A.2d 364 (1984); *Hawthorne v State*, 408 So.2d 801 (1982). For common-law husbands: *People v Torres*, 488 N.Y.S.2d 358 (1985). For boyfriends or lovers: *Smith v State*, 247 Ga. 612, 277 S.E.2d 678 (1981); *State v Anaya*, 438 A.2d 892 (1981).
25. 787 S.W.2d 308 (1990).
26. *Id.* at 309.

27. *Id.* at 310.
28. *Id.* at 312.
29. *Id.* at 311.
30. *People v Romero*, 10 Cal.App.4th 1150, 13 Cal.Rptr.2d 332 (1992), *rev. granted* 17 Cal.Rptr.2d 120, 846 P.2d 702 (1993).
31. *Id.* at 333–334, 340.
32. Nowhere in the case is the term "victim" used to describe Debra. However, the court does make several references to her "suffering" and details her injuries, as well as discussing the possibility that she suffers from battered woman syndrome (*Id.* at 333, 335). Although the term itself is not used, the court paints a fairly obvious picture of the defendant as a victim.
33. *Id.* at 339.
34. *Id.* at 338.
35. *People v Romero*, 13 Cal.Rptr.2d 332, 338 (1992).
36. *State v Lambert*, 312 S.E.2d 31 (1984); *United States v Marenghi*, 893 F.Supp. 85 (1995); *United States v Brown*, 891 F.Supp. 1501 (1995).
37. 893 F.Supp. 85 (1995).
38. *Id.* at 96.
39. This final element of the victimization defense strategy is not always evident or explicit. Although some legal scholars and cases themselves explicitly describe these defendants as victims, such direct characterization is not always used (at least, not to the same extent as in battered women's self-defense cases). Thus, the presence of this element is sometimes tenuous. To some extent, this may account for the limited success of the strategy in these cases.
40. Before the use of the term "post-traumatic stress disorder" in the 1980 *DSM-III* and its subsequent formalization into a defense strategy, a number of defendants attempted to draw a similar war-crime connection in their defenses. In other words, before 1980 several defendants tried to explain their criminal actions, and thereby relieve themselves of responsibility, by arguing that their war experiences had impaired their mental capabilities, causing them to commit the crimes. However, in most of these cases the court denied that a defendant's past war experiences should be taken into consideration when judging his present behavior. See *Bradley v United States*, 447 F.2d 264 (1971); *Harvey v State*, 468 S.W.2d 731 (1971); *Houston v State*, 602 P.2d 784 (1979); *People v Danielly*, 202 P.2d 18 (1949); *People v Walker*, 201 P.2d 6 (1949).

 In two cases, the court did accept the defense's theory that the defendant's behavior was the product of past war trauma: *People v Lisnow*, 88 Cal.App.3d Supp.21, 151 Cal.Rptr. 621 (1978); and *State v Jerrett*, 307 S.E.2d 339 (1983).
41. *State v Felde*, 422 So.2d 370 (1982), *cert. denied*, 103 S.Ct. 1093 (1983); *State v Sharpe*, 418 So.2d 1344 (1982); *State v Simonson*, 669 P.2d 1092 (1983); *Stader v State*, 453 N.E.2d 1032 (1983); *State v Crosby*, 713 F.2d 1066 (1983); *Norris v State*, 490 So.2d 839 (1986); *Stout v State*, 528 N.E.2d 476 (1988).

42. 860 F.Supp. 201 (1994). This case also represents another extension of the use of the strategy to a male defendant.
43. *Id.* at 206–207.
44. *Id.* at 216.
45. *State v Morgan*, 536 N.W.2d 425 (1995).
46. 376 S.E.2d 740 (1989). This case also exemplifies the expanded use of the strategy to men and to acquaintances.
47. *Id.* at 741.
48. *Id.* at 742.
49. *Id.* at 744–745.
50. 860 F.Supp. 201 (1994).
51. *State v Hodges*, 716 P.2d 563 (1986); *Rogers v State*, 616 So.2d 1098 (1993); *Bechtel v State*, 840 P.2d 1 (1992); *State v Janes*, 850 P.2d 495 (1993) [a battered child self-defense case].

6   Moments of Redefinition in Law and Culture

1. However, this inclusion of evidence about the social sources of the psychological trauma is what makes it a "new" defense approach. As discussed in chapter 3, traditional defenses based on psychological impairment did not require any consideration of the causes of that impairment. In fact, testimony about such causes was often excluded. The reliance on testimony about the social causes of the psychological trauma in the victimization defense strategy does make it a new approach that injects a degree of social determinism into the law. However, this is not a complete "triumph of the sociological" because the impact of those social causes must be understood in terms of the more accepted psychological model. In other words, the victimization defense strategy does not assert that social victimization directly causes certain behaviors. Instead, the argument is that in some cases social victimization affects perceptions, which in turn results in certain behaviors.

2. The tendency to think of these two statuses as mutually exclusive was highlighted recently by the O.J. Simpson case. Although Simpson did not rely on the victimization defense strategy in his defense in the killing of his ex-wife Nicole and her friend Ron Goldman, his defense team did attempt to reconstruct Simpson as a victim. They argued that he was a victim of a police conspiracy, rather than of past abuse or suffering. The courtroom struggle unfolded along these lines: Simpson was a victim of a police frame-up, and was therefore innocent of all charges, or Simpson was *not* a victim of a frame-up (because there was no frame-up), and therefore was guilty. At no point did either side (or any commentators) consider that Simpson could be both the offender and a victim of police misconduct, also a possibility. I am not arguing that this is the case. But this is a good example of the social tendency to treat "offender" and "victim" as mutually exclusive categories—Simpson must be either one or the other.

3. An analysis of the use of the victimization defense strategy in other areas of the criminal law could further bolster this point. For exam-

ple, the strategy has been used in sentencing hearings to mitigate responsibility and punishment: *United States v Gaviria*, 804 F.Supp. 476
(1992); *United States v Johnson*, 956 F.2d 894 (1992); *United States v
Hall*, 71 F.3d 569 (1995). An analysis of clemency proceedings could
also be telling. For information on clemency in battered women's
cases, see the *Annotated Bibliography* published by the National
Clearinghouse for the Defense of Battered Women (1996).

References

Abrahamson, Alan. 1993a. "Effects of Menendez Abuse Told." *Los Angeles Times* (14 October):B1, 2.

———. 1993b. "Abuse 'Rewired' Menendez's Brain, Expert Testifies." *Los Angeles Times* (20 October):B1, 5.

Alfieri, Anthony V. 1995. "Defending Racial Violence." *Columbia Law Review* 95:1301–1342.

Alldridge, Peter. 1984. "Brainwashing as a Criminal Law Defence." *Criminal Law Review*:726–737.

Amato, Joseph A. 1990. *Victims and Values: A History and a Theory of Suffering*. New York: Greenwood Press.

American Law Institute. 1985. *Model Penal Code*. Philadelphia, Pa.: The Institute.

Anon. 1986. "The Cultural Defense in the Criminal Law." *Harvard Law Review* 99:1293–1311.

Arenella, Peter. 1993. "Should the Law Blame the Victim Who Takes Revenge?" *Los Angeles Times* (3 August):B9.

Baumann, Mary A. 1983. "Expert Testimony on the Battered Wife Syndrome: A Question of Admissibility in the Prosecution of the Battered Wife for the Killing of her Husband." *Saint Louis University Law Journal* 27:407–435.

Bazelon, David L. 1976a. "The Morality of the Criminal Law." *Southern California Law Review* 49:385–405.

———. 1976b. "The Morality of the Criminal Law: A Rejoinder to Professor Morse." *Southern California Law Review* 49:1269–1274.

Becker, Howard S. 1963. *Outsiders*. New York: Free Press.

Bianchi, Suzanne M., and Daphne Spain. 1986. *American Women in Transition*. New York: Russell Sage Foundation.

Birnbaum, Jesse. 1991. "Crybabies: Eternal Victims." *Time* 138 (12 August):16–18.

Black, Donald. 1976. *The Behavior of Law*. New York: Academic Press.

———. 1989. *Sociological Justice*. New York: Oxford University Press.

Bochnak, Elizabeth, ed. 1981a. *Women's Self-Defense Cases: Theory and Practice*. Charlottesville, Va.: Michie Co.

———. 1981b. "Case Preparation and Development." In *Women's Self-Defense Cases*, edited by Elizabeth Bochnak, 41–85. Charlottesville, Va.: Michie Co.

Bonnie, Richard J. 1995. "Excusing and Punishing in Criminal Adjudication: A Reality Check." *Cornell Journal of Law and Public Policy* 5:1–17.

Bricker, Denise. 1993. "Fatal Defense: An Analysis of Battered Woman's Syndrome Expert Testimony for Gay Men and Lesbians who Kill Abusive Partners." *Brooklyn Law Review* 58:1379–1437.

Brotherton, Geraldine L. 1981. "Post-Traumatic Stress Disorder—Opening Pandora's Box?" *New England Law Review* 17:91–117.

Browne, Angela. 1987. *When Battered Women Kill*. New York: Free Press.

Buechler, Steven M. 1990. *Women's Movements in the United States: Woman Suffrage, Equal Rights, and Beyond*. New Brunswick, N.J.: Rutgers University Press.

Burke, Edward J. 1980. "The 'Bombshell' Defense." *National Law Journal* 2:1, 26.

Butler, Paul. 1995. "Racially Based Jury Nullification: Black Power in the Criminal Justice System." *The Yale Law Journal* 105:677–725.

Chafetz, Janet Saltzman, and Anthony Gary Dworkin. 1986. *Female Revolt: Women's Movements in World and Historical Perspective*. Totowa, N.J.: Rowman & Allanheld.

Chambliss, William J. 1964. "A Sociological Analysis of the Law of Vagrancy." *Social Problems* 12:67–77.

Chicago Tribune. 1994. "Bobbitt Ruled Temporarily Insane when She Cut Husband." (22 January):1, 3.

Child, Irvin L., Elmer H. Potter, and Estelle M. Levine. 1960. "Children's Textbooks and Personality Development: An Exploration in the Social Psychology of Education." In *Human Development: Selected Readings*, edtied by Morris L. Haimowitz and Natalie Reader Haimowitz, 292–305. New York: Thomas Y. Crowell Co.

Cipparone, Rocco C. 1987. "The Defense of Battered Women Who Kill." *University of Pennsylvania Law Review* 135:427–452.

Copp, Kimberly M. 1995. "Black Rage: The Illegitimacy of a Criminal Defense." *John Marshall Law Review* 29:205–238.

Corse, Sarah. 1996. *Nationalism and Literature: The Politics of Culture in Canada and the United States*. Cambridge, U.K.: Cambridge University Press.

Coughlin, Anne M. 1994. "Excusing Women." *California Law Review* 82:1–93.

Crawford, Ian. 1994. "Jury Still Out on Strategy in Bobbitt Case." *Chicago Tribune* (22 January):1, 1+.

Davis, J. Michael. 1976. "Brainwashing: Fact, Fiction and Criminal Defense." *University of Missouri at Kansas City Law Review* 44:438–479.

Delaney, Kevin J. 1992. *Strategic Bankruptcy*. Berkeley: University of California Press.

Delgado, Richard. 1979. "Ascription of Criminal States of Mind: Toward a Defense Theory for the Coercively Persuaded ('Brainwashed') Defendant." *Minnesota Law Review* 63:1–33.

———. 1985. " 'Rotten Social Background': Should the Criminal Law Recognize a Defense of Severe Environmental Deprivation?" *Law and Inequality* 3:9–90.

D'Emilio, Joann. 1985. "Battered Woman's Syndrome and Premenstrual Syndrome: A Comparison of Their Possible Use as Defenses to Criminal Liability." *St. John's Law Review* 59:558–587.

Dershowitz, Alan M. 1994a. *The Abuse Excuse.* Boston: Little, Brown & Co.

———. 1994b. "The Abuse Excuse." *San Francisco Chronicle* (16 January):A15.

Diagnostic and Statistical Manual of Mental Disorders. 1980. 3d ed. Washington, D.C.: The American Psychiatric Association.

———. 1987. Revised 3d ed. Washington, D.C.: The American Psychiatric Association.

Diamond, Bernard L. 1973. "From Durham to Brawner, A Futile Journey." *Washington University Law Quarterly*:109–125.

Dressler, Joshua. 1979. "Professor Delgado's 'Brainwashing' Defense: Courting A Determinist Legal System." *Minnesota Law Review* 63:335–360.

———. 1987. *Understanding Criminal Law.* Oakland, Calif.: Matthew Bender & Co.

———. 1989. "Exegesis of the Law of Duress: Justifying the Excuse and Searching for Its Proper Limits." *Southern California Law Review* 62:1331–1386.

Dror, Yehezkel. 1968. "Law and Social Change." In *The Sociology of Law,* edited by Rita James Simon, 663–680. San Francisco: Chandler Publishing.

Dupps, David S. 1991. "Battered Lesbians: Are They Entitled to a Battered Woman Defense?" *Journal of Family Law* 29:879–899.

Durkheim, Emile. [1933] 1984. *The Division of Labor in Society.* New York: Free Press.

———. 1972. *Selected Writings.* Translated and edited by Anthony Giddens.Cambridge, U.K.: Cambridge University Press.

Erlinder, C. Peter. 1983. "Post-Traumatic Stress Disorder, Vietnam Veterans and the Law: A Challenge to Effective Representation." *Behavioral Sciences and the Law* 1:25–50.

———. 1984. "Paying the Price for Vietnam: Post-Traumatic Stress Disorder and Criminal Behavior." *Boston College Law Review* 25:305–347.

Etzioni, Amitai. 1993. *The Spirit of Community: Rights, Responsibilities, and the Communitarian Agenda.* New York: Crown.

Ewing, Charles Patrick. 1987. *Battered Women Who Kill.* Lexington, Mass.: Lexington Books.

Faigman, David L., and Amy J. Wright. 1997. "The Battered Woman Syndrome in the Age of Science." *Arizona Law Review* 39:67–115.

Falk, Patricia J. 1996. "Novel Theories of Criminal Defense Based on the Toxicity of the Social Environment: Urban Psychosis, Television Intoxication, and Black Rage." *North Carolina Law Review* 74:731–811.

Federal Rules of Evidence. 1989. St. Paul, Minn.: West Publishing.

Feinberg, Joel. 1970. *Doing & Deserving: Essays in the Theory of Responsibility.* Princeton, N.J.: Princeton University Press.

Flaherty, Francis. 1995. "Criminals Are Victims of a Violent Environment." In *Crime and Criminals: Opposing Viewpoints*, edited by Paul A. Winters, 33–38. San Diego: Greenhaven Press.

Fletcher, George P. 1978. *Rethinking Criminal Law*. Boston: Little, Brown & Co.

———. 1988. *A Crime of Self-Defense*. New York: Free Press.

———. 1994. "Convicting the Victim." *New York Times* (7 February):A17.

———. 1995. *With Justice for Some*. New York: Addison-Wesley.

Fox, Sanford J. 1963. "Physical Disorder, Consciousness, and Criminal Liability." *Columbia Law Review* 63:645–668.

Frazier, Patricia A., and Eugene Borgida. 1992. "Rape Trauma Syndrome." *Law and Human Behavior* 16:293–311.

Freeman, Jo. 1975. *The Politics of Women's Liberation*. New York: Longman.

———. 1977. "Resource Mobilization and Strategy: A Model for Analyzing Social Movement Organization Actions." In *The Dynamics of Social Movements*, edited by Mayer N. Zald and John D. McCarthy, 167–189. Cambridge, Mass.: Winthrop.

Friedan, Betty. 1963. *The Feminine Mystique*. New York: Norton.

Friedman, Lawrence M. 1985. *Total Justice*. Boston: Beacon Press.

Gabel, Peter, and Paul Harris. 1982. "Building Power and Breaking Images: Critical Legal Theory and the Practice of Law." *New York University Review of Law and Social Change* 11:369–411.

Gamson, William A. 1987. "Introduction." In *Social Movements in an Organizational Society*, edited by Mayer N. Zald and John D. McCarthy, 1–7. New Brunswick, N.J.: Transaction Books.

Garbarino, James. 1995. *Raising Children in a Socially Toxic Environment*. San Francisco: Jossey-Bass.

Geertz, Clifford. 1983. *Local Knowledge: Further Essays in Interpretive Anthropology*. New York: Basic Books.

Giddens, Anthony, ed. 1972. *Emile Durkheim: Selected Writings*. Cambridge, Mass.: Cambridge University Press.

Gillespie, Cynthia K. 1989. *Justifiable Homicide: Battered Women, Self-Defense, and the Law*. Columbus: The Ohio State University Press.

Glendon, Mary Ann. 1987. *Abortion and Divorce in Western Law*. Cambridge, Mass.: Harvard University Press.

———. 1989. *The Transformation of Family Law*. Chicago: University of Chicago Press.

———. 1991. *Rights Talk: The Impoverishment of Political Discourse*. New York: Free Press.

Glover, Jonathan. 1970. *Responsibility*. New York: Humanities Press.

Goldberg, Stephanie B. 1994. "Fault Lines." *ABA Journal* (June):40–44.

Goldman, Lauren E. 1994. "Nonconfrontational Killings and the Appropriate Use of Battered Child Syndrome Testimony: The Hazards of Subjective Self-Defense and the Merits of Partial Excuse." *Case Western Reserve Law Review* 45:185–249.

Goldstein, Joseph, and Jay Katz. 1963. "Abolish the 'Insanity Defense'—Why Not?" *Yale Law Journal* 72:853–876.

Goodwin, Merrilee R. 1996. "Parricide: States Are Beginning to Recognize that Abused Children who Kill their Parents Should be Afforded the

Right to Assert a Claim of Self-Defense." *Southwestern University Law Review* 25:429–460.

Greenawalt, Kent. 1984. "The Perplexing Borders of Justification and Excuse." *Columbia Law Review* 84:1897–1927.

———. 1986. "Distinguishing Justifications from Excuses." *Law and Contemporary Problems* 49:89–126.

Greenberg, Jack. 1994. *Crusaders in the Courts*. New York: Basic Books.

Gregory, Sophronia Scott. 1994. "Oprah! Oprah in the Court!" *Time* 143 (6 June):30–31.

Grier, William H., and Price M. Cobbs. 1968. *Black Rage*. New York: Basic Books.

Gross, Hyman. 1973. "Some Unacceptable Excuses." *Wayne Law Review* 19:997–1005.

Grossman, Joel B., and Mary H. Grossman, eds. 1971. *Law and Change in Modern America*. Pacific Palisades, Calif.: Goodyear.

Gusfield, Joseph R. 1986. *Symbolic Crusade: Status Politics and the American Temperance Movement*. Chicago: University of Illinois Press.

Hagan, John. 1980. "The Legislation of Crime and Delinquency: A Review of Theory, Method, and Research." *Law and Society Review* 14:603–628.

Hall, Jerome. 1952. *Theft, Law and Society*. Indianapolis: The Bobbs-Merrill Co.

Hamblin, Ken. 1994. "Watch Your Back and Don't Trust Anyone." *Denver Post* (24 April):F3.

Harris, Paul. 1977. "Black Rage: Political Psychiatric Defenses." In *Frontier Issues in Criminal Litigation*, 95–98. Los Angeles: People's College of Law.

———. 1997. *Black Rage Confronts the Law*. New York: New York University Press.

Hart, H.L.A. 1968. *Punishment and Responsibility*. New York: Oxford University Press.

Hole, Judith, and Ellen Levine. 1971. *Rebirth of Feminism*. New York: Quadrangle Books.

———. 1989. "The First Feminists." In *Feminist Frontiers II: Rethinking Sex, Gender, and Society*, edited by Laurel Richardson and Verta Taylor, 437–444. New York: Random House.

Hollinger, Richard C., and Lonn Lanza-Kaduce. 1990. "The Process of Criminalization: The Case of Computer Crime Laws." In *Criminal Behavior*, 2d ed., edited by Delos H. Kelly, 29–43. New York: St. Martin's Press.

Holstein, James A., and Gale Miller. 1990. "Rethinking Victimization: An Interactional Approach to Victimology." *Symbolic Interaction* 13:103–122.

Hughes, Robert. 1993. *Culture of Complaint*. New York: Oxford University Press.

Hunter, Edward. 1952. *Brainwashing in Red China Chinese*. Hsiang-Kang: Tung fang chou pan she.

Jacobs, Joanne. 1994. "Abuse is No Excuse for Mutilation or Murder." *Atlanta Journal* (21 January):A12.

Kadish, Sanford H. 1976. "Respect for Life and Regard for Rights in the Criminal Law." *California Law Review* 64:871–901.

———. 1987. "Excusing Crime." *California Law Review* 75:257–289.

Kakutani, Michiko. 1994. "A Lawyer Warns about Vigilantism." *New York Times* (27 September):C19.

Kaminer, Wendy. 1995. *It's All the Rage*. Reading, Mass.: Addison-Wesley.

Kempe, C. Henry, et al. 1962. "The Battered-Child Syndrome." *Journal of the American Medical Association* 181:17–24.

Kessler-Harris, Alice. 1982. *Out to Work: A History of Wage- Earning Women in the United States*. New York: Oxford University Press.

Kieviet, Thomas G. 1978. "The Battered Wife Syndrome: A Potential Defense to a Homicide Charge." *Pepperdine Law Review* 6:213–229.

Kotake, Donna L. 1993. "Survey: Women and California Law." *Golden Gate University Law Review* 23:1069–1080.

Krause, Harry D. 1995. *Family Law in a Nutshell*. St. Paul, Minn.: West Pub.

Krauss, Elissa, and Beth Bonora. 1983. *Jurywork: Systematic Techniques*. 2d ed. New York: Clark, Boardman, and Callaghan.

LaFave, Wayne R., and Austin W. Scott Jr. 1986. *Criminal Law*. 2d ed. St. Paul, Minn.: West Publishing.

Lefcourt, Carol H., ed. 1995. *Women and the Law*. New York: Clark, Boardman, and Callaghan.

Leo, John. 1988. "The Dubious Art of Shifting Blame." *U.S. News & World Report* 105 (17 October):68.

———. 1990. "The It's-Not-My-Fault Syndrome." *U.S. News & World Report* 108 (18 June):16.

———. 1992a. "A 'Victim' Census for Our Times." *U.S. News & World Report* 113 (23 November):22.

———. 1992b. "The Psychologizing of Crime." *U.S. News & World Report* 113 (7 December):22.

———. 1994. "Watching 'As the Jury Turns'." *U.S. News & World Report* 116 (14 February):17.

Lewis, Neil A. 1994. "Justice Thomas Assails Victim Mentality." *New York Times* (17 May):A14.

Lindesmith, Alfred R. 1965. *The Addict and the Law*. Bloomington: Indiana University Press.

Luker, Kristin. 1984. *Abortion and the Politics of Motherhood*. Berkeley: University of California Press.

Lukes, Steven, and Andrew Scull, eds. 1983. *Durkheim and the Law*. Oxford: Martin Robertson.

Lunde, Donald T., and Thomas E. Wilson. 1977. "Brainwashing as a Defense to Criminal Liability: Patty Hearst Revisited." *Criminal Law Bulletin* 13:341–382.

Macaulay, Stewart, et al., eds. 1995. *Law & Society: Readings on the Social Study of Law*. New York: Norton.

Mackinnon, Catharine A. 1989. *Toward a Feminist Theory of the State*. Cambridge, Mass.: Harvard University Press.

Macpherson, Susie, et al. 1981. "Expert Testimony." In *Women's Self-Defense Cases*, edited by Elizabeth Bochnak, 87–105. Charlottesville, Va.: Michie Co.

Magnet, Myron. 1995. "The Culture of Personal Irresponsibility Causes Crime." In *Crime and Criminals: Opposing Viewpoints*, edited by Paul A. Winters, 67–76. San Diego: Greenhaven Press.

Maguigan, Holly. 1991. "Battered Women and Self-Defense: Myths and Misconceptions in Current Reform Proposals." *University of Pennsylvania Law Review* 140:379–486.

Mauro, Tony. 1994. "Abuse as an Excuse Raises Public Outcry." *USA Today* (8 February):1A.

McCarthy, John D., and Mayer N. Zald. 1987. "Resource Mobilization and Social Movements: A Partial Theory." In *Social Movements in an Organizational Society*, edited by Mayer N. Zald and John D. McCarthy, 15–42. New Brunswick, N.J.: Transaction Books.

McNulty, Faith. 1980. *The Burning Bed*. New York: Harcourt Brace Jovanovich.

McQuiston, John T. 1994. "A Novel Insanity Defense for Joel Rifkin." *New York Times* (26 July):B1+.

Milloy, Courtland. 1994. "Self-Defense Goes Insane in the City." *Washington Post* (18 May):D1, 6.

Mills, Nicolaus. 1994. "The Shame of 'Black Rage' Defense." *Chicago Tribune* (6 June):Section 1, 13.

Milton, Pat. 1995. "Long Island Killer Gets 6 Life Terms." *Boston Globe* (23 March):3.

Monahan, John, and Laurens Walker. 1994. *Social Science in Law*. 3d ed. Westbury, N.Y.: Foundation Press.

Moore, Michael S. 1985. "Causation and the Excuses." *California Law Review* 73:1091–1149.

Moreno, Joelle Anne. 1989. "Killing Daddy: Developing a Self-Defense Strategy for the Abused Child." *University of Pennsylvania Law Review* 137:1281–1307.

Morris, Norval. 1968. "Psychiatry and the Dangerous Criminal." *Southern California Law Review* 41:514–547.

———. 1982. "The Criminal Responsibility of the Mentally Ill." *Syracuse Law Review* 33:477–531.

Morrow, Lance. 1991. "A Nation of Finger Pointers." *Time* 138 (12 August):14–15.

Morse, Stephen J. 1976. "The Twilight of Welfare Criminology: A Reply to Judge Bazelon." *Southern California Law Review* 49:1247–1268.

———. 1978. "Crazy Behavior, Morals, and Science: An Analysis of Mental Health Law." *Southern California Law Review* 51:527–654.

———. 1985. "Excusing the Crazy: The Insanity Defense Reconsidered." *Southern California Law Review* 58:777–836.

Ms. (spring 1972):113.

National Clearinghouse for the Defense of Battered Women. 1996. *Annotated Bibliography*. Philadelphia, Pa.

Newsweek (23 March 1970):71–78.

Nolan, James L. Jr. 1998. *The Therapeutic State: Justifying Government at Century's End*. New York: New York University Press.

Norrie, Alan. 1983. "Freewill, Determinism and Criminal Justice." *Legal Studies* 3:60–73.

Note. 1981. "Cults, Deprogrammers, and the Necessity Defense." *Michigan Law Review* 80:271–311.

O'Donnell, William, and David A. Jones. 1982. *The Law of Marriage and Marital Alternatives*. Lexington, Mass.: Lexington Books.

Okun, Lewis. 1986. *Woman Abuse: Facts Replacing Myths*. New York: State University of New York Press.

Olson, Walter K. 1991. *The Litigation Explosion: What Happened When America Unleashed the Lawsuit*. New York: Dutton.

Page, Clarence. 1994. "Black Rage: A Defense for the Times." *Chicago Tribune* (29 May):Section 4, 3.

Parsons, Talcott, and Robert F. Bales. 1955. *Family, Socialization and Interaction Process*. Glencoe, Ill.: Free Press.

Peele, Stanton. 1989. *Diseasing of America: Addiction Treatment Out-of-Control*. Lexington, Mass.: Lexington Books.

Pillsbury, Samuel H. 1992. "The Meaning of Deserved Punishment: An Essay on Choice, Character, and Responsibility." *Indiana Law Journal* 67:719–752.

Platt, Anthony M. 1977. *The Child Savers*. Chicago: University of Chicago Press.

Pleck, Elizabeth. 1987. *Domestic Tyranny: The Making of Social Policy Against Family Violence from Colonial Times to the Present*. New York: Oxford University Press.

Press, Andrea Lee. 1991. *Women Watching Television: Gender, Class, and Generation in the American Television Experience*. Philadelphia: University of Pennsylvania Press.

Raifman, Lawrence J. 1983. "Problems of Diagnosis and Legal Causation in Courtroom Use of Post-Traumatic Stress Disorder." *Behavioral Sciences and the Law* 1:115–130.

Richardson, James T. 1996. " 'Brainwashing' Claims and Minority Religions Outside the United States: Cultural Diffusion of a Questionable Concept in the Legal Arena." *Brigham Young University Law Review* 1996:873–904.

Rieff, David. 1991. "Victims All?" *Harper's Magazine* 283:49–56.

Rieff, Philip. 1987. *The Triumph of the Therapeutic*. Chicago: University of Chicago Press.

Robinson, Haddon W. 1994. "Call Us Irresponsible." *Christianity Today* 38:15.

Robinson, Paul H. 1982. "Criminal Law Defenses: A Systematic Analysis." *Columbia Law Review* 82:199–291.

Rosen, Cathryn Jo. 1986. "The Excuse of Self-Defense: Correcting a Historical Accident on Behalf of Battered Women Who Kill." *The American University Law Review* 36:11–56.

Ross, Alf. 1975. *On Guilt, Responsibility and Punishment*. Berkeley: University of California Press.

Rothman, Sheila M. 1978. *Woman's Proper Place: A History of Changing Ideals and Practices, 1870 to the Present*. New York: Basic Books.

Ryan, Barbara. 1992. *Feminism and the Women's Movement*. New York: Routledge.

Saario, Terry N., Carol Nagy Jacklin, and Carol Kehr Tittle. 1973. "Sex

Role Stereotyping in the Public Schools." *Harvard Educational Review* 43:386–416.

Schneider, Elizabeth M. 1980. "Equal Rights to Trial for Women: Sex Bias in the Law of Self-Defense." *Harvard Civil Rights-Civil Liberties Law Review* 15:623–647.

———. 1986a. "The Dialectic of Rights and Politics: Perspectives from the Women's Movement." *New York University Law Review* 61:589–652.

———. 1986b. "Preface." *Women's Rights Law Reporter* 9:191–193.

———. 1986c. "Describing and Changing: Women's Self-Defense Work and the Problem of Expert Testimony on Battering." *Women's Rights Law Reporter* 9:195–222.

Schneider, Elizabeth M., and Susan B. Jordan. 1978. "Representation of Women Who Defend Themselves in Response to Physical or Sexual Assault." *Women's Rights Law Reporter* 4:149–163.

———. 1981. "Representation of Women Who Defend Themselves in Response to Physical or Sexual Assault." In *Women's Self-Defense Cases*, edited by Elizabeth Bochnak. Charlottesville, Va.: Michie Co.

Schudson, Michael. 1989. "How Culture Works." *Theory and Society* 18:153–180.

Schuller, Regina A., and Neil Vidmar. 1992. "Battered Woman Syndrome Evidence in the Courtroom." *Law and Human Behavior* 16:273–291.

Schulz, Justin W. 1982. "Trauma, Crime and the Affirmative Defense." *The Colorado Lawyer* 11:2401–2406.

Scrignar, C. B. 1988. *Post-Traumatic Stress Disorder*. 2d ed. New Orleans: Bruno Press.

Skeen, David. 1983. "The Genetically Defective Offender." *William Mitchell Law Review* 9:217–265.

Slade, Margot. 1994. "At the Bar." *The New York Times* (20 May):B20.

Slovenko, Ralph. 1984. "The Meaning of Mental Illness in Criminal Responsibility." *The Journal of Legal Medicine* 5:1–61.

Smith, Susan C. 1992. "Abused Children Who Kill Abusive Parents: Moving Toward an Appropriate Legal Response." *Catholic University Law Review* 42:141–178.

Sneirson, Judd F. 1995. "Black Rage and the Criminal Law: A Principled Approach to a Polarized Debate." *University of Pennsylvania Law Review* 143:2251–2288.

Staples, Brent. 1994. "The Rhetoric of Victimhood." *The New York Times* (13 February):4, 14.

Steadman, Henry, et al. 1993. *Before and After Hinkley: Evaluating Insanity Defense Reform*. New York: Guilford Press.

Steele, Shelby. 1990. *The Content of Our Character: A New Vision of Race in America*. New York: St. Martin's Press.

Studer, Marlena. 1984. "Wife Beating as a Social Problem: The Process of Definition." *International Journal of Women's Studies* 7:412–422.

Sutherland, Edwin. 1950. "The Diffusion of Sexual Psychopath Laws." *American Journal of Sociology* 56:142–148.

Sykes, Charles J. 1992a. *A Nation of Victims: The Decay of the American Character*. New York: St. Martin's Press.

———. 1992b. "Oh, Say, Can We Whine." *Chicago Tribune Magazine* (20 September):16–21.

Sykes, Gresham M., and Francis T. Cullen. 1992. *Criminology*. 2d ed. New York: Harcourt Brace Jovanovich.

Taylor, John. 1991. "Don't Blame Me!" *New York* 24 (3 June): 26–34.

———. 1994. "Irresistible Impulses, Why America Has Lost Its Capacity to Convict the Guilty." *Esquire* 121:96–98.

Thompson, B. Carter. 1986. "Defending the Battered Wife." *Trial* 22 (February):74–80.

Tierney, Kathleen J. 1982. "The Battered Women Movement and the Creation of the Wife Beating Problem." *Social Problems* 29:207–220.

Tomasic, Roman. 1985. *The Sociology of Law*. London: Sage Publications.

The Trial of Patty Hearst. 1976. San Francisco: The Great Fidelity Press.

Vago, Steven. 1994. *Law & Society*. 4th ed. Englewood Cliffs, N.J.: Prentice-Hall.

Van Sambeek, Mavis J. 1988. "Parricide as Self-Defense." *Law and Inequality* 7:87–106.

Vermeire, Albert R. 1981. " 'Deprogramming': From the Defense Counsel's Perspective." *West Virginia Law Review* 84:91–134.

Volpp, Leti. 1994. "(Mis)Identifying Culture: Asian Women and the 'Cultural Defense'." *Harvard Women's Law Journal* 17:57–101.

Vuoso, George. 1987. "Background, Responsibility, and Excuse." *The Yale Law Journal* 96:1661–1686.

Walker, Lenore E. 1979. *The Battered Woman*. New York: Harper & Row.

———. 1984. *The Battered Woman Syndrome*. New York: Springer.

———. 1989. *Terrifying Love*. New York: Harper & Row.

———. 1993. "Battered Women as Defendants." In *Legal Responses to Wife Assault*, edited by N. Zoe Hilton, 233–257. London: Sage Publications.

Weinreb, Lloyd L. 1986. "Desert, Punishment, and Criminal Responsibility." *Law and Contemporary Problems* 49:47–80.

Weitzman, Lenore J. 1979. *Sex Role Socialization*. Mountain View, Calif.: Mayfield Publishing.

———. 1981. *The Marriage Contract: Spouses, Lovers, and the Law*. New York: Free Press.

———. 1985. *The Divorce Revolution: The Unexpected Social and Economic Consequences for Women and Children in America*. New York: Free Press.

Wellborn, Jack Jr. 1982. "The Vietnam Connection: Charles Heads' Verdict." *Criminal Defense* 9:7–19.

Wilson, James Q. 1997. *Moral Judgment: Does the Abuse Excuse Threaten Our Legal System?* New York: Basic Books.

Women on Words & Images. 1975. *Dick and Jane as Victims: Sex Stereotyping in Children's Readers*. Princeton, N.J.

Wright, R. George. 1994. "The Progressive Logic of Criminal Responsibility and the Circumstances of the Most Deprived." *Catholic University Law Review* 43:459–504.

Cases Cited

B

Bechtel v State, 840 P.2d 1 (1992).
Borders v State, 433 So.2d 1325 (1983).
Bradley v United States, 447 F.2d 264 (1971).

C

Commonwealth v Bruno, 407 A.2d 413 (1979).
Commonwealth v Craig, 783 S.W.2d 387 (1990).
Commonwealth v Kacsmar, 617 A.2d 725 (1992).
Commonwealth v Miller, 634 A.2d 614 (1993).
Commonwealth v Stonehouse, 555 A.2d 772 (1989).
Commonwealth v Watson, 494 Pa. 467, 431 A.2d 949 (1981).
Commonwealth v Zenyuh, 307 Pa.Super. 253, 453 A.2d 338 (1982).

D

Daubert v Merrell Dow Pharmaceuticals, Inc., 509 U.S. 579 (1993).
Durham v United States, 214 F.2d 862 (1954).
Dyas v United States, 376 A.2d 827 (1977).

F

Freeman v People, 4 Denio 9 (N.Y. Sup.Ct. 1847).
Frye v United States, 293 F. 1013 (1923).

G

Glass v Vaughn, 860 F.Supp. 201 (1994).
Green v Scully, 850 F.2d 894 (1988).

H

Harvey v State, 468 S.W.2d 731 (1971).

Hawthorne v State, 408 So.2d 801 (1982).
Houston v State, 602 P.2d 784 (1979).

I

Ibn-Tamas v United States, 407 A.2d 626 (1979), *reversed and remanded*, 455 A.2d 893 (1983), *aff'd.*

J

Jahnke v State, 682 P.2d 991 (1984).

M

M'Naghten's Case, 10 Cl. & F. 200, 8 Eng. Rep. 718 (1843).

N

Neelley v State, 494 So.2d 669 (1985).
Norris v State, 490 So.2d 839 (1986).

P

People v Cruickshank, 105 A.D.2d 325, 484 N.Y.S.2d 328 (1985).
People v Danielly, 202 P.2d 18 (1949).
People v Ewing, 72 Cal.App.3d 714, 140 Cal.Rptr. 299 (1977).
People v Giacalone, 242 Mich. 16, 217 N.W. 758 (1928).
People v Hoover, 187 Cal.App.3d 1074, 231 Cal.Rptr. 203 (1986).
People v Humphrey, 921 P.2d 1 (1996).
People v Jackson, 18 Cal.App.3d 504, 95 Cal.Rptr. 919 (1971).
People v Lisnow, 88 Cal.App.3d Supp. 21, 151 Cal.Rptr. 621 (1978).
People v Manson et al., 61 Cal.App.3d 102, 132 Cal.Rptr. 265 (1976).
People v Minnis, 118 Ill.App.3d 345, 455 N.E.2d 209 (1983).
People v Otis, 174 Cal.App.2d 119, 344 P.2d 342 (1959).
People v Patrick, 541 P.2d 320 (1975).
People v Powell, 102 Misc.2d 775, 424 N.Y.S.2d 626 (1980), *aff'd* 83 A.D.2d 719, 442 N.Y.S.2d 645 (1981).
People v Romero, 10 Cal.App.4th 1150, 13 Cal.Rptr.2d 332 (1992), *rev. granted* 17 Cal.Rptr.2d 120, 846 P.2d 702 (1993).
People v Sexton, 31 Ill.App.3d 593, 334 N.E.2d 107 (1975).
People v Torres, 488 N.Y.S.2d 358 (1985).
People v Walker, 201 P.2d 6 (1949).
People v Wilson, 194 Mich.App. 599, 487 N.W.2d 822 (1992).

R

Rogers v State, 616 So.2d 1098 (1993).

S

Smith v State, 247 Ga. 612, 277 S.E.2d 678 (1981), *on remand* 159 Ga.App. 183, 283 S.E.2d 98 (1981).
Stader v State, 453 N.E.2d 1032 (1983).
State v Allery, 101 Wash.2d 591, 682 P.2d 312 (1984).
State v Anaya, 438 A.2d 892 (1981).
State v Crigler, 23 Wash.App. 716, 598 P.2d 739 (1979).
State v Crosby, 713 F.2d 1066 (1983).
State v Elsea, 251 S.W.2d 650 (1952).
State v Felde, 422 So.2d 370 (1982), *cert. denied*, 103 S.Ct. 1093 (1983).
State v Felton, 329 N.W.2d 161 (1983).
State v Fields, 376 S.E.2d 740 (1989).
State v Gachot, 609 So.2d 269 (1992), *cert. denied*, 114 S.Ct. 478 (1993).
State v Hadley, 65 Utah 109, 234 P. 940 (1925).
State v Hill, 287 S.C. 398, 339 S.E.2d 121 (1986).
State v Hodges, 239 Kan. 63, 716 P.2d 563 (1986).
State v Holden, No. 49566, slip op. (Ohio Ct. App. Sept.26, 1985).
State v Hundley, 236 Kan. 461, 693 P.2d 475 (1985).
State v Jacoby, 260 N.W.2d 828 (1977).
State v Janes, 121 Wash.2d 220, 850 P.2d 495 (1993).
State v Jerrett, 307 S.E.2d 339 (1983).
State v Kelly, 97 N.J. 178, 478 A.2d 364 (1984).
State v Lambert, 312 S.E.2d 31 (1984).
State v Leidholm, 334 N.W.2d 811 (1983).
State v Loss, 295 Minn. 271, 204 N.W.2d 404 (1973).
State v Morgan, 536 N.W.2d 425 (1995).
State v Nuetzel, 606 P.2d 920 (1980).
State v Pagano, 242 S.E.2d 825 (1978).
State v Reid, 747 P.2d 560 (1987).
State v Sharpe, 418 So.2d 1344 (1982).
State v Simonson, 669 P.2d 1092 (1983).
State v Trombino, 352 So.2d 682 (1977).
State v Wanrow, 88 Wash.2d 221, 559 P.2d 548 (1977).
State v Wilkins, 407 S.E.2d 670 (1991).
State v Williams, 787 S.W.2d 308 (1990).
State v Wright, 112 Iowa 436, 84 N.W. 541 (1900).
Stout v State, 528 N.E.2d 476 (1988).

T

Terry v State, 467 So.2d 761 (1985).

U

United States v Alexander and Murdock, 471 F.2d 923 (1973).
United States v Batchelor, C.M. 377832, 19 C.M.R. 452 (1954).
United States v Brawner, 471 F.2d 969 (1972).
United States v Brown, 891 F.Supp. 1501 (1995).

United States v Dickenson, 6 U.S.C.M.A. 438, 20 C.M.R. 154 (1955).
United States v Fishman, 743 F.Supp. 713 (1990).
United States v Gaviria, 804 F.Supp. 476 (1992).
United States v Hall, 71 F.3d 569 (1995).
United States v Hearst, 424 F.Supp. 307 (1976).
United States v Hearst, 563 F.2d 1331 (1977).
United States v Johnson, 956 F.2d 894 (1992).
United States v King et al., 840 F.2d 1276 (1988).
United States v Marenghi, 893 F.Supp. 85 (1995).
United States v Olson, 7 U.S.C.M.A. 460, 22 C.M.R. 250 (1957).
United States v Patrick, 532 F.2d 142 (9th Cir. 1976).
United States v Schneider, Cr. No. 74–241 SC (N.D. Cal. 1975).
United States v Thomas and Richards, 11 F.3d 1392 (1993).

W

Walsh v People, 88 N.Y. 458 (1882).
Washington v United States, 390 F.2d 444 (1967).
Whipple v State, 523 N.E.2d 1363 (1988), *habeas corpus denied, Whipple v State*, 957 F.2d 418, *cert. denied*, 113 S.Ct. 218 (1992).

Index

About the Author

Saundra D. Westervelt is an assistant professor of sociology at the University of North Carolina at Greensboro. She teaches criminology and the sociology of law. Her previously published works include analyses of scientific fraud, "Fraud and Trust in Science" (with Stephan Fuchs), and of the images of crime in reality-based TV programming, "The World of Crime According to *Cops*" (with Paul Kooistra and John Mahoney). She is currently working on a sociological analysis of the post-conviction review process and the cases of defendants who have been exonerated by that process.